Capital Transformation and Privatization in Hungary

István Tamás, Ph.D.

VANTAGE PRESS
New York

Published by Vantage Press, Inc.
516 West 34th Street, New York, New York 10001

Manufactured in the United States of America
ISBN: 0-533-12877-3

Library of Congress Catalog Card No.: 98-90669

0 9 8 7 6 5 4 3 2 1

Contents

List of Tables

List of Figures

Foreword

The idea to write this thesis one day and publish it in book form came up after he opened his mail sometime in the autumn of 1989. "Upheaval in the East," read a headline in one of America's daily newspapers. "I smiled briefly that morning," explained Hungarian Professor István Tamás almost a decade later. "I knew the real upheaval was yet to come." He referred to the painful process of privatization and capitalization, by far his country's most important historical development since Russian troops crushed Hungary's revolution against Soviet domination in 1956.

"The Hungarian Revolution against Stalinism was as much a fight for a free market economy as it was for democracy," recalled Tamás. And in 1989 and 1990, politicians finally decided to continue the process of privatization and capitalization, which began in the '80s. Once sacred, state-owned companies, got new owners. Coca-Cola, Pepsi-Cola, Pizza Hut, and McDonald's brand names soon appeared on buildings where bullet holes were still evidence of Hungary's darker hours. Small Hungarian business owners began painting their drab homes and decorating their shop windows.

Encouraged by privatization, Hungary's private sector grew at a spectacular pace through the creation of new enterprises. It also became clear that in comparison with a typical market economy, the Hungarian enterprise sector would be characterized by a large proportion of very small companies for years to come. But Tamás had his doubts about the reemergence of Hungary's long oppressed, entrepreneurial spirit. "I realized that the euphoria could fade away, and that entrepreneurs could need help to cope with the new situation," argued Hungary's leading economist.

So, in 1989, he started one of Hungary's first venture capital and investment companies called Dunaholding Plc., named after the Danube, the river which inspired so many artists and professionals. Dunaholding Plc. began helping Hungarian employees and others interested in the privatization of state-owned companies. "I wanted to help Hungarian enterprises in their difficult but exciting transformation into new, competitive, firms,"

Tamás said. Six short years later, he became director-general of Hungary's largest private college, the International Business School-Budapest (IBS).

Although Hungary has a long tradition of high educational standards, many state-run schools are currently facing a period of budgetary constraints, which slows down the required reforms. In addition, many former Communist teachers find it hard to adjust to the new era of change. Some of them openly criticized private schools and tried to influence the authorities not to acknowledge diplomas from these "new institutions." Tamás was not surprised. "It is true that education centers such as the Karl Marx University changed their names and colors," he admitted, "but the old way of thinking did not disappear. That is one of the reasons why we began with our own school."

IBS and Dunaholding Plc. gave him the necessary insights to investigate the privatization process in this country. But Tamás realized he would not make many friends among certain politicians after publishing the results of his research of the 1987–1997 period, because he concluded that Hungarian privatization "had not achieved its initial goals" completely.

"I wanted to give an honest picture about Hungary, which initiated the reforms throughout Central and Eastern Europe," Tamás told me. "Capital transformation and privatization in Hungary" is therefore a window to one of the world's fastest developing and emerging markets. This is a handbook for investors and everyone interested in this beautiful, inspiring nation, accompanied by an overview of the largest state-owned companies participating in privatization.

It is also a remarkable, brave, and intellectual work about the success stories and failures of a country of ten million, which still attracts more foreign investments than any other former East Block state. The Budapest Stock Exchange (BSE), which continued its operation in 1990 after more than four decades of Communist rule, is another indicator of Hungary's dramatic transformation. What started as a small, almost insignificant institution with weekly meetings and one quoted share, grew into the world's fastest expanding bourse.

By early 1996, less than six years after its official opening, forty-one companies were listed at the BSE. Share capitalization on the stock market tripled since the end of 1994, and the value of average monthly trading in shares increased by 300 percent in the first few months of 1995. Tamás spent much time explaining this phenomenon and the reasons why privatization and restructuring have gone further in Hungary than in most economies in transition. In sectors such as telecommunications and energy supply, the private involvement is greater than those of many European Union member states.

Tamás also investigated the reasons behind the 15.25 billion dollars Foreign Direct Investment (FDI) Hungary received from the United States, Great Britain, Germany, Austria, France, Italy, and the Netherlands until the end of 1996. An estimated fifty percent of that amount was spent on greenfield investments, which contributed to the technological renewal of Hungarian industries. But despite much praise from international organizations such as the World Bank, Tamás saw that there was also another story, less popular, to tell.

And unlike most of his colleagues who are afraid to "tarnish" Hungary's image abroad, Tamás did not hide the mistakes made in this last historic decade of economic reforms. For example, he discovered that Hungarian privatization "had not entirely achieved its goal of reorganizing the major part of Hungarian industry" by selling it to foreign investors. The reason? Foreigners found Hungarian privatization "slow" and "complicated." Also, Hungary's external debt could not be reduced substantially by privatization revenues.

In addition, Tamás saw that all post-Communist governments of Hungary missed a golden opportunity. "The privatization was to create a proprietary group that was supposed to lay down the basis of a new middle-class. This goal has only be achieved to a small extent. . . . " These problems, combined with the stress of a new market economy and the disappearance of cradle-to-grave security, can lead to social unrest.

And then there were the scandals which, by many accounts, overshadowed the now almost completed privatization process from day one. The battle of (Communist) officials to keep their positions, properties, and power lead to serious problems. They participated in what Tamás described as "spontaneous privatization," or the transformation of state-owned companies into thousands of new companies. "When such enterprises were transformed into companies, state-owned assets could be sold well under the market value," he explained to me, showing me the script of his book.

He realized that his factual, well-researched work would not be welcomed by those involved in shady, financial dealings. "But I cannot keep silent," Tamás added. As late as in 1990, Hungary's last Communist government decided to tackle the problem of spontaneous privatization by introducing legislation regarding the protection of state assets, and the scope of privatization. But by that time, at least 100 billion Hungarian forints (almost 500 million dollars) were already transferred into companies.

And when everybody thought that everything was said and done, a new public and political debate began about the return of properties to their former owners. Under Communism, millions of people lost everything they had worked for; homes, factories, land, money, and even furniture and jewelry. It was perhaps fair to assume that as part of privatization and denationalization, these people had the right to receive at least some of their properties back.

But in a dramatic move, the government of the early '90s decided to sell those properties to outside investors, while giving the original owners no more than some (financial) compensation. Even some state-owned farms around Lake Balaton and vineyards in the famous Tokaj wine region were purchased by outside investors. Supporters of radical parties suggested that Hungary was sold out to foreigners and former Communists. Despite these tensions, the controversial sale of properties continued.

Perhaps the controversies could have been prevented. However, Professor István Tamás did not give up hope. "Despite the still weak financial system, an increasing number of domestic investors are involved in the privatization process. These companies stand a good chance of playing a significant role in Hungary and its neighboring countries," Tamás noted.

When he received his Ph.D from Newport University, he thought about his three children. "They were and are my motivation to write this thesis," he said, "I believe the next generation will overcome the mistakes of the past, and build a better future for our country. I will do everything I can to help these youngsters." This book will surely help them to reflect on Hungary's most turbulent years of the late twentieth century.

Stefan J. Bos

Stefan J. Bos is a Dutch journalist who has worked and lived in Hungary since 1989. He currently works as the Budapest-based Central Europe correspondent for several newspapers and broadcasting networks including CBS News Radio, Deutsche Welle, Voice of America, and Belgium's Flemish Radio and Television (VRT). In 1997, Bos received the "Correspondent of the Year '97" from former minister of foreign affairs, Laszlo Kovacs, for his coverage of Hungarian foreign policy.

Capital Transformation and Privatization in Hungary

1

The Main Periods of Hungarian Privatization

The year of the change of regime, 1990, was a real turning point in the history of ownership in Hungary. In the 1957–90 period, all moves relating to ownership structure were made against the prevailing ideology. This was also true of the household farm plots institutionalized at the beginning of the 1960s, when the agricultural pressure groups could have their way in spite of political and administrative opposition, resulting in the official authorization of household plots. The comment is also valid in the case of the 1968 economic reform, which tried to make the economy more efficient by reforming state-owned enterprise at a time when enterprise reformation was a taboo topic. In spite of this, subsidiary enterprises of agricultural cooperatives (co-ops) appeared on the scene as by-products of the 1968 reform. These ventures were actually the next phase of the development of private capital in Hungary. In 1982, the government approved the introduction of nine new legal forms of private enterprise. However, the goal was not to reform ownership and build a private sector against the state sector but rather to try to improve the functioning of an economy that had deteriorated alarmingly in the 1970s.

During the 1980s, the political leadership made a series of attempts to curtail private capital that started to appear in the form of small enterprises. The economic revitalization program introduced, in 1985, attempted to improve the position of state-owned large-scale industry and other large state-owned enterprises. Even then the tacit goal was to strengthen state ownership, because by that time the rapid accumulation of private capital within small enterprises had started to threaten the positions of state-owned enterprises. It is no coincidence that in 1987–88 spontaneous privatization began, using authorized legal forms for the transfer from state ownership into private hands. Although spontaneous privatization could only produce a trickle of private ownership, and the asset management holdings thus created were not yet true private ownership forms, nonetheless it could already indicate the symptoms of internal decay, which was so rampant in state ownership.

The history of Hungarian privatization is simultaneously that of denationalization and the creation of a private sector. Starting in 1957, the Hungarian economy almost continuously, at first with furtive steps, then in 1968 taking a giant leap and in the 1980s decisively and massively, moved closer and closer to the creation of a free market and the accumulation of private investment capital. As I interpret the term *privatization* in the narrow sense (i.e., the sale of state-owned assets to private owners), I understand that the *building of a private sector* and *denationalization* are significantly wider terms than *privatization.* Privatization in the narrow sense was and is a relatively fast-paced process, linked partly to the beginning of spontaneous privatization starting around 1987 and partly to the creation of the legal and institutional framework introduced immediately prior to and after the 1990 change of regime. Denationalization and the creation of the private sector is historically a much longer and deeper process.

In Hungary, the private capital accumulation, denationalization, and privatization processes have always been accompanied by a sort of "cat-and-mouse" game, in which the state initially dislikes but tolerates the creation of a private sector that slips the control of the state. Then a new government comes to power, focusing its ideology around the development of the fledgling private sector, and this government wishes to exert centralized control over the privatization processes, leading to the expansion of this private sector. The processes of controlled and non-controlled private capital accumulation have been present in the Hungarian economy since 1957. These processes could have played an important part in driving the socialist economy, already increasingly less centralized and planned, closer and closer toward spontaneous market building and the spontaneous degradation of state assets.

1. History of Privatization

Three major processes can be considered as antecedents of the privatization process unfolding in the second half of the 1980s. Of these, the oldest in time was the household plot system, introduced as a result of the battle fought by agricultural pressure groups in the beginning of the 1960s.

2

The household plot system, which incorporated the traditions of agricultural Hungary, was the first serious crack in the wall of the centrally planned economic system. At the peak of its operation, the household plots employed 3 million part-time workers, bypassed all central controls or ministry directives, and operated in a fully decentralized manner based on independent decisions. At first, politicians and top administrators were unwilling to institutionalize the household plot system, but then they were forced to do so by the concerted efforts of agricultural pressure groups and certain county-level political leaders. It was the first time since 1956 that the politicians had to yield and make concessions to the system's elite, the elite of a dictatorship created at the end of the 1940s. Of course, these political concessions were well calculated and simultaneously well defined. They failed to cover the industrial and service sectors and remained limited both in size and sphere of activity. Still, the household plot system constituted an autonomous and more or less independent island within a centrally planned economic environment.

The second phase of denationalization, including the creation of the private sector, was brought about by the 1968 economic reform. Although the 1968 economic reform lacked any ownership concept and failed to tackle any transformation of the administrative organization or the state-owned enterprise system, it still managed to open up another loophole. It allowed the creation of subsidiary enterprises within co-ops, which then stopped performing any agricultural activity and operated as manufacturers of goods or rendered services instead. The private economy expanded within the framework of an agrarian economy but had already started to move toward the industrial and service sectors. The entry of co-ops into the domestic market affected the competitive status of state-owned industries and services much more than the very limited competition of private retailers and craftsmen. Although in the 1970s there were renewed attacks against the subsidiary enterprises of agricultural co-ops, these remained—until the 1982 legislation on small-scale enterprise—as the gradually expanding basis of the creation of the private sector.

While the private sector enterprise forms introduced at the beginning of the 1960s and in 1968 were the result of pressure exerted by the agricultural political lobbies, the government made a voluntary concession in 1982 with the introduction of nine new legal forms of small-scale private enterprise. The reason for this concession was the debt service burden resulting from the foreign loans raised in the 1970s. By the end of the 1970s, the debt service burden was such that in 1977–78 the political leadership

3

itself decided on the cautious restart of market reforms. In this framework, a price reform was introduced in 1980, followed by the famous regulation stipulating the nine new legal forms in 1982.

The economic history of the 1980s signals accurately that this had stopped being just a fumbling about and a massive restructuring process had begun. New companies, incorporated according to the new legal forms, soon covered the whole country. Set up in state-owned large-scale industry and services and in strengthened private enterprises in agriculture, they very soon raised real competition against state enterprises that had been in a monopolistic position in the domestic market until then. This competition was wage-based competition, since small-scale enterprises could pay much higher wages that their state-owned counterparts. This resulted in a brain drain, a flow of leading experts from the state-owned enterprises to private companies. In 1985, partly because of this brain drain, state-owned industry started a counterattack, trying to improve its weakening positions by introducing a recovery program. However, the recovery program lost steam within eighteen months. State-owned industry realized that it was now impossible to maintain domestic market positions with unchanged organizational and compensation forms.

2. Spontaneous Privatization (1988–90)

We call the first phase of the privatization process spontaneous privatization. During this phase, state-owned industry reorganized horizontally structured internal divisions and units into a company format (joint stock or limited liability). First, the headquarters of the enterprise was transformed to become an asset management organization and then, in the next phase, a company. This path was followed by state-owned large enterprises that got into a difficult financial position in the 1980s. These enterprises were usually heavily in debt and received no grants during the 1985 recovery program. To solve the complicated situation, they chose the formula of flight forward, hoping to slow down the further accumulation of losses by separating divisions and units from headquarters, which formula could also enable them to handle debts better, in a decentralized manner. The enterprises also expected to pay higher wages through the new company format, thus ensuring stronger individual and group commitment. At the same time, the financial regulations conferred a series of advantages

4

with the transformation of internal units into a company form. The transformation process was also motivated by the acquisition of these advantages.

Until 1990, the history of privatization, denationalization, and the creation of the private sector could be characterized by the weakest link principle: It was always the weakest link that was authorized to leave the nationalized system. The creation of the private sector started with agriculture, because food was one of the most important strategic commodities for politicians: the safe supply of food to the population was part of the limited legitimization of the system. Even the 1982 legislation on small-scale enterprise was based on the weakest opposition, the weakest link principle: only small-scale private enterprises could be set up, with strict limits on employee numbers. The entire regulation was explicitly against organizational growth. At the start of spontaneous privatization it could also be seen that the first initiatives were made by large enterprises that lacked enough clout in the administrative market of the state to have access to additional investment and wage payment sources. Thus, spontaneous privatization was started by enterprises in the instrument and light industry sectors, being in a weaker bargaining position, and not by the largest and strongest enterprises in the heavy industry, mining, or machine manufacturing sectors.

Even in the later stages of privatization, when the apparent sequence was reversed and the new government presented privatization as the focus of both its ideology and its action program, large state-owned enterprises with strong bargaining positions were not included. The only exception in the privatization program of the first four years was MATÁV (Magyar Tavközlési Vállalat) whose political weight was smaller than its actual economic weight. The market value of its assets and the revenue expected from its partial sale neutralized all opposition to the sale. When looking at the privatization cases of the first four years, we see that the absence of the largest utility enterprises and five out of the six largest state-owned commercial banks is apparent. The first privatization package, started in 1990, included twenty enterprises that were considered the best and most attractive for foreign investors. But when we look at the market position, asset status, or political clout of these twenty enterprises, the conclusion is that these are not in the same class as the "really big ones" mentioned earlier.

That feature remained unchanged in the later phases of controlled and centrally guided privatization: the stronger the position of a state-owned

5

enterprise in the market or the state administration, or in both, the less its inclination to participate in the "adventure" of privatization.

3. The Phase of Controlled and Centrally Guided Privatization (1990–92)

Prior to the change of regime in May 1990, the Németh government had set up the State Property Agency (SPA). The main goal of this agency was to check and curtail uncontrolled state asset degradation that went on under the guise of spontaneous privatization. During the spontaneous privatization process, the management of state-owned enterprises set up thousands of new companies. When such enterprises were transformed into companies, state-owned assets could be sold at least in part, well under market value. If the privatization process is uncontrolled, it is impossible to say whether such sales were on or under market value. During the spontaneous privatization period, state assets worth more than 100 billion forints were transferred into companies. The magnitude of this transfer roused public opinion, causing suspicion and anger. At the same time, the dissolution of state-owned enterprises into a loose cluster of companies became part of a peculiar denationalization process, because the new companies depended on state institutions in a very indirect manner. In a not negligible part of the cases, the state-owned enterprises became decentralized and at the same time privatized.

The measures of the leading officials of the Németh government taken to curtail spontaneous privatization were based on well-defined modernization principles. The essence of these was that neither employees nor managers were considered capable of being good owners. Practically no additional development sources could be expected, other than from abroad; thus spontaneous privatization should be stopped and the sale of state assets to foreigners should become the priority instead. Of course, the administration was also sensitive to the reactions of public opinion, pointing at abuses committed in the name of spontaneous privatization.

As election time was approaching, the government could not afford to be seen as the tacit supporter of squandering of state assets. As a result, the last government of the old regime promulgated two laws. Act No. 7 of 1990, on the protection of state assets entrusted to enterprises, and Act No. 8 of 1990, on the SPA. These acts concentrated all competence relating to

6

transformation and privatization in the SPA, thus curtailing the playing ground of enterprises and strengthening controls.

The starting position of the privatization phase 1990–92 was largely determined by the dispute on the privatization strategy conducted within the new government coalition. The Independent Small Farmers' Party wished to reclaim all formerly nationalized assets and transfer title to their earlier proprietors, including not only land but also apartments, factories, and all other property. The other two parties of the coalition preferred privatization and compensation (to be paid to the earlier proprietors) to reprivatization. The dispute was ended by the decision of the Constitutional Court prohibiting any discrimination among earlier proprietors according to the type of property (land, real estate, factory, or other property). This decision made impossible a compromise among the coalition partners who had planned to offer complete restitution to ex-landowners while paying only compensation to the earlier proprietors of all other assets. The result of the decision was the compensation system, in which there was no legal difference among nationalized assets, although the institution of land auctions did create a technical difference between land and other assets. In spite of the differences of opinion on the privatization-reprivatization issue and within this land restitution, the coalition managed to overcome the problem within a very short time, and, in addition to the compensation process, privatization could begin in earnest.

The SPA was, at first, supervised by Parliament, but in the summer of 1990 the government decided to put the SPA under government supervision. Although the government decision caused political disputes, privatization thus avoided becoming the focus of political battles within Parliament.

If a Parliament committee had supervised the SPA and had privatization transactions got in the crossfire of daily Parliament disputes, the privatization body could hardly have dealt with professional and technical questions. Finally, government supervision meant that the privatization disputes, charged with politics and occasionally also with passions and emotions, did not get into direct contact with the daily decisions of the privatization body. Thus, these daily decisions could be based on professional grounds. This was helped by the government inviting the representatives of the opposition parties to participate in the eleven-member board of directors of the SPA.

The main product of the centrally controlled and guided privatization process of the 1990–92 period was the transformation of enterprises.

7

Thirty percent of state-owned enterprises were transformed into companies, and 10 to 15 percent of them were privatized. However, a significant part of the increasing number and value of transformations was only formal and could be regarded as administrative. This was especially true of large-scale enterprises. In this phase, foreign direct investments (FDI) played a very significant role, in spite of the fact that the twenty most promising enterprises of the first privatization program could not be sold. Still, true change of ownership and almost 75 percent of privatization revenue were attributable to foreign investors during this phase. In 1992, however, after the very active role played in 1990 and 1991, the participation of FDI became dramatically smaller. This suggested that the boom of FDI concentrated first of all on medium-sized companies; foreign investment activity in small-scale enterprises or big industry was almost negligible. At that time, the main aim of foreign investors was to acquire a significant shareholding, business shares below 30 percent being uncharacteristic. The higher the absolute amount of the FDI, the stronger the will of the new foreign owner to acquire majority ownership position.

Looking back at this phase of privatization from a 1997 vantage point, it can be said now that the assumption that state-owned enterprises transformed into companies become transparent and therefore more attractive to (mainly foreign) investors proved to be wrong. For this assumption to be valid, a more appropriate structure, a better supply of companies, and a domestic economic climate more favourable to investment would probably have been necessary. In reality, the enterprise transformation process occurring in 1990–92 prolonged rather than helped privatization, because it gave the semblance of an enterprise moving toward privatization by its assuming the legal form of a company. In fact, the main result of the first two years of the centrally controlled and guided privatization process was not the preparation of state-owned companies for privatization but, on the contrary, the loss of a significant part of their assets. Thus they were devalued continuously and at an accelerated pace in the eyes of investors. The intention behind both the establishment of the SPA and the enacting of the Transformation Act was to curtail and control spontaneous privatization and the tricks of company managers turning state ownership into private property. The prolongation of obligatory transformation, however, finally caused damage to the cause of privatization. By the end of 1992, state-owned companies that had been marketable in 1990 found themselves in a deteriorating asset and market situation, rendering investment in them unattractive.

4. The Phase of Preferential Privatization (1992–94)

The legislation (Acts 53, 54, and 55) enacted in 1992 separated the so-called temporary and permanent assets of the state, and all related responsibilities were allocated to two separate organizations. Enterprises listed in a separate government decree now belonged to the State Property Holding Company (SPH). Only a certain number of these enterprises (later companies) could be privatized, as stipulated by the decree. The rest of the enterprises remained with the SPA; these were to remain in state hands only for the time being (in so-called "temporary" state ownership).

The law stipulated deadlines for the transformation of both types of enterprises. Through this, state-owned enterprises lost the remainder of their independence: earlier, they had been the authors of their own privatization; now they had become objects of a privatization process. Roughly two-thirds of state assets managed earlier by the SPA were transferred to the SPH.

The Employee Share Ownership Program (ESOP) was also approved in 1992. Through this, employee organizations of state-owned companies could also become participants in privatization. The ESOP also tried to solve the problem of manager buyouts, legally not existing at that time, by functioning as a form of management buyout (MBO). The approval of the ESOP reflects the change of government philosophy. Earlier the government had excluded any approach except market-type privatization, supplemented by the compensation system and a series of preferences offered to investors. Now the government clearly tried to boost the demand side of privatization by the introduction of the ESOP and later by other preferential privatization techniques such as the Small-Scale Investor Share Ownership Program. This change of philosophy made clear that the government had become aware that the process of privatization so far had prevented the creation of a strong middle class, a new bourgeoisie. If privatization went on like that, without preferences and applying only market method, then—if one ignores the new owners of catering and retail units sold in the preliminary privatization program—no significant new capitalist class would be created in Hungary. This government turnabout of political motivation was a feature of the political situation halfway between two elections; now the government seemed to be aware it had only two more years until the new elections. So far, privatization had been unable to create a new capitalist class that could become the mainstay of its political

9

support. New privatization techniques had to be attempted. In 1993, the so-called Small-Scale Investor Share Purchase Program (KRP) was approved, which offered significant state support to small-scale investors, who, as citizens, would have the right to participate in the purchase of state assets. In the framework of this program, a single initial public offering (IPO) was organized in the first half of 1995, amounting to 5 billion forints.

5. 1995—The Forced March of Privatization

Between mid-1994 and the spring of 1995, Hungarian privatization was in a state of suspended animation. It did not come to a halt, but the number of privatization transactions was very low. The reasons were the elections, followed by the internal privatization disputes of the new government. By the end of 1995, however, the preparations to complete the most important transactions in the history of Hungarian privatization were completed. The Hungarian power industry, the gas distribution industry, a large part of the oil and gas industry, and a major block of shares of the telecommunication industry (MATÁV) were put up for sale for foreign state-owned strategic investors.

As a consequence of the huge transactions completed at the end of 1995, the Treasury obtained its largest revenue ever from privatization. In a single year, 1995, it received 450 billion forints, mostly through sales to foreign direct investors. It is not the objective of this study to enumerate the arguments against the rash and needlessly forced privatization of the power industry. In a few years' time it would be clear that it was wrong to sell off the Hungarian power sector to foreign strategic investors and the huge revenue of 1995 was essentially unnecessary from the aspect of macroeconomic stabilization.

6. Completion of Privatization

According to the Privatization Act, the privatization process must be completed before the end of 1997. It is expected that some transactions will be protracted, and these will be completed only in the first half of 1998. As the privatization process in Hungary was started in 1988 and should be completed before the end of 1998, privatization will have taken the greater part of a decade. Privatization will continue with municipality-owned enterprises, and after 1998 the municipalities can be regarded as the main protagonists of the decentralized privatization process. The market value of assets owned by almost 3,200 municipalities (utility enterprises, land, blocks of shares, etc.) is very difficult to estimate. In addition, these assets are expected to upgrade continuously after 1998, when the Hungarian economy is expected to have passed the transformation crisis and to achieve first a modest, then an impressive economic growth rate.

2

Changing Privatization Objectives and Methods

In 1990, the new government defined the basic goal of privatization: the dominance of state ownership in the competitive sphere should be terminated and a private sector created, which would perform the basic restructuring of the economy. The new leadership planned the privatization of 50 to 60 percent of state ownership within three or four years. This meant that privatization was based partly on ideology and partly on empirical experience, accepting that private property could be operated more efficiently than state-owned property. Due to privatization, a competitive private sector was to be created, and this private sector would have the double task of economic restructuring and the directing of Hungarian foreign trade toward the markets of developed countries. At that time, privatization was seen as the key element of transition to a market economy.

In spite of the absence of fast privatization, the creation of efficient forms of state asset management never materialized. Although the SPH was the owner, it never really acted as such, and the enterprises fell into an "ownership vacuum," receiving almost no instruction from the state that could tell them how to operate or prepare for privatization.

1. Modernization, Revenue Maximization, and Social Justice

In addition to modernization objectives, two other main objectives of similar importance appeared in the first phase of privatization: revenue maximization and social justice. The government hoped to collect a privatization revenue, which could help to alleviate the serious social burden of the transition period and finance infrastructure investments absolutely necessary for the modernization of the country. Social justice partly meant compensation paid for nationalized property and partly equal chances for the different groups of society in the competition for assets to be privatized. In the 1990–92 period, revenue maximization was not an important issue, as the trade balance showed a surplus. Although the budget deficit deteriorated significantly compared with IMF instructions, the deficit could easily be financed even without large privatization revenues. In the 1992–94 period, however, privatization revenues started to gain special importance; the large budget deficit had to be financed, and the government wanted to see privatization revenues flowing in. These circumstances made possible, even urgent, the privatization of MATÁV at the end of 1993. A revenue in excess of $U.S. 800 million made a significant contribution to the reduction of the budget deficit.

The government wanted to enforce social justice to compensate for the past and to help people in the future. It preferred compensation for nationalized property to reprivazation. This solution was probably better than full restitution (i.e., returning all nationalized assets to their original owners, which in most cases would have been impossible and in other cases could have generated complicated legal disputes) but was not a perfect solution as far as social justice was concerned. Although compensation was allotted to almost 1 million earlier owners, it was impossible to pay compensation for four decades of revenue not generated by confiscated property, for lost lifestyle, or for lack of a family existence that could be a base for a safe future. Another problem for social justice was that the bulk of society never received any compensation while, in a certain sense, the previous four decades had caused each member of society to lose something in the area of individual and communal freedom.

During the past periods of privatization, the three main objectives of modernization, revenue maximization, and social justice had never been in harmony with one another. It was only natural that aspects of modernization objectives and social justice would clash. Compensation is not a tool to create a competitive private sector. It cannot achieve an improved position for the Hungarian economy in the world, nor can it make a contribution to successful economic restructuring. Revenue maximization is both practically and theoretically contrary to both modernization objectives and social justice. In order to help the creation of a competitive market economy, privatization revenues should have been pumped back into the economy by means of state-financed infrastructure and other development projects. Instead, they were used to finance the budget deficit, resulting in a withdrawal of funds from the manufacturing sector and infrastructure development, delaying the meeting of modernization objectives. Finally, financing the budget deficit with privatization revenues meant increased consumption, since restriction of demand thus became less severe. Unfortunately, the reallocation of revenues through the state budget occurred mostly in unchanged structures, which meant that this kind of increased spending did little to strengthen the private sector.

2. Partial Objectives of Privatization

In addition to the three main objectives of privatization, other, partial objectives were set. One such partial objective was to allow access to new markets and new capital and the research and development results of the privatizing professional partner to state-owned companies while being privatized. Another objective was the renewal of management. The new owner should sooner or later make additional investments and help his new company have access to the newest technical/technological processes and linkage to a broader network of alliances. Such partial objectives are usually tied to professional, especially foreign, investors. One feature of foreign direct investment in Hungary is that nearly three-quarters of the foreign capital present in privatization has arrived through professional investors. This means that state assets have not been bought up by financial investors who act through the stock exchange, but rather by professional investors who purchased the enterprises and assets offered to them during privatization.

In 1990, another important partial objective of privatization was set. If possible, more professional investors should be attracted to Hungary, thus gaining access to new markets, technologies, management, and other factors that could increase competitiveness. Although in the majority of cases these partial objectives were never met entirely, the presence of foreign professional investors could sometimes produce a series of negative consequences. In many cases the foreign professional investor only wanted to acquire a share in the Hungarian market, and in some cases the foreign professional investor wanted to stop the exports of the Hungarian company, thus protecting his own internal market. Due to the underdevelopment of the stock exchange and the technical problems of evaluating the performance of Hungarian companies through the stock market, a major role of financial investors could not be reckoned with. Either professional investors had to be chosen to participate in privatization or no foreign investment would come forth.

As mentioned earlier, privatization in the whole 1990–94 period lacked a true privatization strategy supported by a uniform set of objectives. Compared with the other countries of the region, the main feature of Hungarian privatization was the absence of a dominant privatization model, the ownership structure being transformed simultaneously through several channels. Hungary managed to avoid the pitfalls of gratuitous privatization, and all applied techniques were essentially of a market type, based on competition. Most privatizers were professional investors, and the proportion of foreign capital in privatization was high, reaching almost 50 percent of revenues.

3. Privatization Revenue and Capital Loss

Until mid-1997, the total revenue collected from privatization can be considered as significant, reaching almost $U.S. 5 billion. This revenue helped to reduce the budget deficit and contributed to a small extent to the modernization of companies and the improvement of their liquidity position. At the same time, the shortsighted focus on revenues of Hungarian privatization slowed down the privatization process and neglected such tasks as direct company investments or those aiming at the creation of new jobs, thus sidetracking the long-term privatization objectives. As opposed to privatization in East Germany, in Hungary the creation of new jobs never enjoyed a higher priority than revenues. Although there were several privatization transactions where the state prescribed the meeting of certain employment obligations, the first priority always remained state income. Even then, the prescriptions relating to employment were never complied within a significant number of cases.

When assessing the status of Hungarian privatization, one should compare the revenues—which at first seem significant—with the capital loss of companies, the amount of which is much higher than that of privatization revenues. Most household savings were of a pecuniary nature, kept partly in Hungary and partly abroad (which was assumed to increase). Only a negligible amount of these funds was used for investment during privatization. This was unfortunate, because one of the most dramatic and successful economic tendencies of the past four years was the skyrocketing of household savings. If we add to these savings the probable flight of foreign capital, it is clear that in the first half of the 1990s Hungary had an extremely high savings rate, even when compared with the best savers of the world. The household savings rate could be put at 12 to 15 percent, but most of the money avoided privatization and ended up as financial savings and—to a smaller extent—as private investments.

4. Privatization and the Strategies of Foreign Capital

Due to the quick-changing nature of privatization, in the first phase (1990–94) the success could not be used abroad for the enhancement of the country's image. In the 1988–92 period, Hungary had a clear advantage in the region and was regarded as the front runner among the former COMECON (Council for Mutual Economic Assistance) countries. Due to this, in the 1990–91 period foreign investors were hugely interested in investments in Hungary.

This was especially true in connection with privatization investments, because at that time foreign investors intended—in addition to acquiring the Hungarian markets of state-owned enterprises—to use Hungary as a springboard for their expansion to the rest of the ex-COMECON countries. But from the end of 1991 or the beginning of 1992 the modification of their strategy became evident.

Foreign investors—disappointed by the privatization methods—chose a new, two-pronged strategy, discarding their earlier interest in the acquisition of Hungarian manufacturing and commercial bases by means of privatization. One branch of this strategy was to set up new manufacturing, commercial, service, and financial bases in Hungary in the form of greenfield investments or by the establishment and later development of new companies. The other branch of the modified strategy was to build individual bases in each ex-COMECON country. Hungary was unable to formulate an investment policy that could handle the Carpathian Basin as a single economic unit. Whereas the Hungarian market is small, comprising only 10 million consumers, the surrounding region has up to 50 or 60 million inhabitants, providing a much larger market for potential investors. The priority of Hungarian investments could have been maintained in the region by the introduction of this "Carpathian Basin as a single economic unit" concept. Even so, Hungary managed to attract more than 50 percent of the foreign capital invested in the region. This was less due to the success of Hungarian privatization policy than to the maturity of the Hungarian corporate and market environment, the advanced legal system, and the flexibility of Hungarian entrepreneurs and employees.

5. Privatization and the Status of the Stock Exchange

One shortcoming of Hungarian privatization was the almost complete ignorance of the capital market. After a four-decade-long suspension, the Budapest Stock Exchange (BSE) reopened its doors on March 21, 1990, being the first stock exchange in the region. However, any deliberate security market or stock exchange development policy was missing.

The first IPO was driven not by any long-term policy but by the wish to gain astronomical profits. The state should have taken a large number of stocks to the reopened BSE and, through the introduction of certain stock regulations, obliged investors to make long-term investments. Unfortunately, the opposite was the case. With some exceptions, the BSE attracted no financial investments at all. Although the BSE has a good standing in the region, the opportunity was lost for it to become the central securities market of the region after Vienna.

In this period, privatization policy also incorporated a small-scale investor program. Deliberate sales of securities to domestic small-scale investors could have attracted foreign financial investors, simultaneously balancing the role of foreign investments by strengthening domestic capitalists. The government started the small-scale investor program as late as 1993, but was unable to acquire even the minimum of social support necessary for the program to succeed.

6. Preferential Privatization Techniques

From 1992 on, Hungarian investors gradually gained ground in privatization, which was mainly due to preferential privatization techniques aimed at reviving domestic privatization demand. A relatively wide range of Hungarian entrepreneurs could acquire property through techniques that were based on open competition or other market-concept methods of public property acquisition. The proliferation of preferential techniques helped to accelerate the privatization process, which had seemed to grind to a halt at the beginning of 1993. In the run-up to the 1994 elections, support of Hungarian investors became more intensive, mostly for political reasons. After the elections, however, support dwindled even faster than the privatization process itself.

In addition to the obstacle of political preference, foreign investors could go shopping for assets elsewhere in Eastern Europe, leaving a significant amount of assets to be privatized unsold.

The first preferential construction to be introduced was the Existence loan (E-loan). In the beginning, the E-loan was quite a clumsy tool, lacking truly attractive conditions. Later the conditions were improved, and by the end of 1994 the SPA had sold assets worth almost 60 billion forints through this method. After 1994 the construction was suspended, to all practical purposes.

The other large-volume preferential construction was asset sale against compensation certificates. At the time of the redemption of the certificates, interest was added to their nominal value. The price of the certificate at the stock exchange was much lower, so for certificate holders there was a significant price advantage. Of course, the true extent of the advantage was heavily influenced by the value of the asset offered against the certificates. This resulted in significant leeway for the seller. By the end of 1994, sales against certificates amounted to almost 50 billion forints. In the 1995–97 period, the real value of sales reached 20 billion forints.

A technique of employee asset acquisition used extensively around the world is the ESOP. This was adapted and introduced also in Hungary. After a clumsy start, it made significant progress in 1993. By the beginning of 1995, a total of 197 companies were sold in this program. The sale of Herend China Factory is frequently mentioned as a brilliant example of the ESOP. On the other hand, we should not forget the case of Nagykanizsa Brewery, whose ESOP organization was soon forced to sell off the freshly privatized company to stronger investors. Doubts still linger on, as the viability of such companies remains uncertain in spite of the active participation of the management. In most cases, additional capital investment never occurred, which was not the case with the withdrawal of profits. After 1994, the ESOP was discontinued.

One tool of delayed payment is leasing, which was also introduced to stimulate privatization. Privatization leasing was applied if at least two unsuccessful bids proved that the given company could not be sold under better conditions. By the end of 1995, twenty-four companies had been sold in this way.

6.1. E-Loans

The E-loan is one of the oldest privatization tools, available to Hungarian investors since 1991. Its awkward construction and the absence of state guarantees were the result of a long duel between the banks and the financial administration (won by the latter), which resulted in the banks' demanding a very high collateral—frequently amounting to 200 percent of the loan granted. Until January 1993, interest in E-loans was scant, but after this date it became the financing base of several privatization techniques. The application of this tool gained ground from the beginning of 1993, when the government introduced positive measures favoring the E-loans. The reduction of E-loan interest rates was obtained by the financial administrations, enlisting the help of the Ministry of Trade. The result was the jump-start of privatization by means of E-loans (and, simultaneously, through the ESOP). Those intending to purchase state assets now had access to loans with even better terms.

The Basic Conditions of the E-Loan

- E-loans could only be used to purchase state-owned shares and only to the extent that the state debt would be repaid.
- The source of the loan was the central bank refinancing credit, the interest consisting of the refinancing rate and the interest margin due to financial institutions.
- One feature of the construction was the exclusive use of cash for the repayment of privatization costs. However, compensation certificates could also be used up to the minimum private resource required.
- The business share purchased under the terms of the loan could not be sold on or brought into a business without the approval of the financial institution. The condition for selling on was that the new owner must also be eligible for the loan. Eligibility is proven when the applicant—or, in case of alienation, the new applicant—satisfies the credit requirements of the lender bank and has the necessary private capital.

The Changing Elements of the E-Loan Construction

The changes primarily affected eligibility. At first, eligibility was restricted to those considered to be Hungarian as far as the foreign exchange

19

regulations were concerned. From 1992 on, private businesses became eligible if considered Hungarian by the foreign exchange regulations.

In the first year of the construction, E-loans could only be used for the purchase of state assets, including state-owned land and state-owned business shares but excluding securities. From 1992 on, E-loans could also be used to purchase securities. The 1993 amendment paved the way for the purchase of state-owned business shares by private businesses.

As a result of the amendment, private businesses set up for the purpose of buyout applied for the E-loans. The financial institution demanded a mortgage covering all the assets of the company, frequently stipulating surety or prompt collection order, eventually also requiring an option to purchase the company.

With the E-loan construction, the government mainly intended to have a suitable financing form for preliminary privatization. As a consequence, in 1991 E-loans were available exclusively for SPA-organized sales. From 1992, however, every state asset management organization could privatize using this financial construction. Even with these preferential loan terms, the conditions of the financial institutions (which usually demanded a collateral amounting to 150 to 200 percent of the loan granted) were a serious obstacle for the applicants. The government decree did not stipulate any collateral, except for the sale of the preliminary privatization lease rights (due to the fact that lease rights are practically impossible to mortgage). When applying for E-loans or privatization loans, compensation certificates were to be taken into consideration at nominal value as private resources.

The practice of each financial institution differed in terms of the acceptable type of collateral and/or the evaluation aspects of the business shares offered.

The establishment of the Credit Guarantee Company allowed a few applicants lacking their own resources to ask for its surety. At the outset, typically retail and catering units were purchased by this means. But by the second half of 1993 major buyouts became a widespread practice. Individual privatization (the auction method) proved to be too clumsy.

In 1993, the use of E-loans in privatization payments grew to 21 percent. This growth was made possible mainly by the easier access to loans. By the beginning of 1995, the total value of E-loans used had reached 62 billion forints, corresponding roughly to 15 percent of all privatization sales thus far.

Some of the banks were sufficiently cautious to require strict adher-

Table 1

Main Terms of E-Loans

Year	Own resources (millions of forints)	Rate	Term (years)	Grace period (years)
1991-92	Below five	2 %	6.5	1
	Between five and ten	15 %	8.0	1
	Above ten	25 %	10.0	2
1993	Below five	2 %	15.0	3
	Above five	15 %	15.0	3

Source: State Property Agency.

ence to their conditions and had a serious credit rating process in place. The debtors owing funds to these banks could usually meet their payment obligations. Even in the minor transactions executed earlier (1992), these cautious banks granted loans only to applicants who had prior knowledge of the state asset to be purchased. If, for example, they had been the lessees, they could accurately know the real business opportunities of the state asset. In some cases, the debt service of the E-loan was even lower than the lease fee paid earlier. Less cautious banks, however, accumulated significant past due interest and principal backlogs. There were cases when the debtor could not even meet its first repayment obligation. Here it is reasonable to assume that the business plan and the whole enterprise were totally groundless, the debtor having no intention whatsoever to re-pay the loan in the first place. This indicated significant shortcomings of banking practices.

Almost half of all E-loans went to trade and a further third to the other service sectors. Area distribution was also quite skewed. Forty percent of loans were taken down in Pest County (including Budapest) and 11 percent in Baranya County, while the share of all other counties was less than 5 percent.

By the end of 1993, the share of E-loans in SPA revenues generated by preliminary privatization was almost 40 percent. By the end of 1994, the same ratio in ESOP sales exceeded 50 percent.

Nineteen commercial banks and two specialized financial institutions participated in the E-loan system. The distribution of E-loans amounting to 49.5 billion forints up to June 30, 1994, by fifteen major lenders, is shown in table 5.

Table 2

Role of E-Loans among the Revenues of the SPA

Year	SPA revenues (billions forints)	E-loans disbursed (billions forints)	E-loans as % of SPA revenues
1991	31.38	1.01	3.2
1992	74.82	9.07	12.2
1993	81.80	21.70	26.5
1994	97.27	30.23	31.1
Feb. 1995	4.72	0.92	19.5
TOTAL	289.90	62.93	21.7

Source: Privatization Research Institute.

The number of banks granting E-loans amounting to less than 500 million forints is much smaller in the total overall. The two largest lenders even incorporated E-loans in their business strategy, attempting to increase their relatively low share of the business sector through E-loans to new customers. These lenders were Agrobank (whose business policy terminated at the end of 1994 with a widely publicized scandal) and—at least until 1993—Postabank. The tendency was also present, to a certain extent, with the OTP (Országos Takarekpéntàr és Kereskedelmi Bank Rt) Bank as well. A general condition prevailing was that the lender offering E-loans would become the debtor's main bank. Agrobank and Postabank, however, wanted to attract new customers by offering them less strict loan conditions, thus "poaching" them from their earlier account-keeping banks (mainly the Commercial Bank, the Credit Bank, and partly the Budapest Bank).

A significant percentage of borrowers used E-loans to purchase stocks. Most of these purchases targeted the privatization of the Danubius hotel chain.

In the course of the preliminary privatization, almost 2,500 entrepreneurs gained access to preferential E-loans. In 1993, the applicant structure underwent a significant change. While until mid-1993 relatively small E-loans (average 1 to 2 million forints) granted for preliminary privatization and share purchase dominated, in the second half of 1993 the average E-loan exceeded 10 million forints. This indicated the use of E-loans for the purchase of acquiring business shares from mid-1993.

The effects of E-loans could be deemed positive because privatization was accelerated, more private companies were set up, and entrepre-

Table 3

The Role of E-Loans in the Individual Privatization Programs
(until December 31, 1994)

	Preliminary privatization*	ESOP	Self-privatization
Total program revenue (billion forints)	15.74	38.50	18.00
Of which E-loans (billion forints)	6.09	22.16	8.13
Share of E-loans in program revenues (%)	38.69	57.55	44.67

* December 31, 1993.

Source: Privatization Research Institute.

Table 4

Distribution of E-Loans According to Size

Loan amount (billion forints)	Number of loans	In % of All E-Loans
0-1	10,681	81.29
1-2	980	7.46
2-3	563	40.80
3-4	315	2.40
4-5	250	1.90
5	378	2.38
Total	**13,140**	**100.00**

Source: Privatization Research Institute

neurs became more sophisticated in the law. At the same time, E-loans were limited to the acquisition of property and no E-loans could be had for the operation of the property (not to mention the debt service burden of these E-loans). As a consequence, the financial position of the new owners could deteriorate and the danger of renationalization loomed. The debt service burden significantly limited the playing ground of these companies. Due to the low levels of private resources, the risk to the entrepreneurs was small. Since they mostly gambled with someone else's money, this could result in the expansion of a negative attitude to entrepreneurs.

There were three basic categories of E-loan borrowers. The first category contained managers and employees who assumed unreasonable risks

Table 5

E-Loan Withdrawal by Banks 1990 - 1994 (June 30) in Billion Forints

	Total
Commercial Bank	6.491
Budapest Bank	4.606
OTP Bank	5.011
Foreign Trade Bank	2.885
General Banking and Trust	659
Postabank	8.502
Iparbankház	926
Agrobank	6.640
Mezőbank	754
Takarékszöv. Bank	511
Credit Bank	5.977
Dunabank	731
Inter-Európa Bank	1.087
Corvinbank	797
Konzumbank	1.749
Total	**49.516**

in an attempt to keep their jobs and former positions. The second category contained the entrepreneurs who, attracted by the favorable conditions, were driven by their "adventurous" nature to buy state assets on credit. This second category had two types. The first type was not interested in the purchased assets at all. He just wanted to gain access to a loan and pump the asset value from the company or eventually launder some illegal revenues. If he was successful, the company would go bankrupt and the owner would gain financially. The second type would like to go into business with almost no capital, possible under this system, but due to the high debt service burden and the weak managerial skills or lack of market knowledge of the owner, the company could go bankrupt. The third category, sensing a good business opportunity and using the preferences, would like

24

to have a solid business in the future.

In the spring of 1995 the E-loan program was discontinued.

6.2. The ESOP

The stimulation of employee ownership is one of the most important tools of preferential ownership acquisition. In many cases, this tool is capable of saving jobs from liquidation. Employees become owners and thus more committed, which can promote the creation of an efficient business. In Hungary (as opposed to the United States) the ESOP was not a participation institution assisting employees to acquire company shares but rather a kind of preferential technique promoting domestic ownership.

In line with the essence of the construction, the program was only suitable for successful companies or those that could be made successful. The loan and installment conditions prevailing in the period when the ESOP was introduced allowed only 8 percent of Hungarian enterprises to be privatized through the ESOP. Pessimists even lowered this figure to 5 percent.

The Legal Framework of Buyout through the ESOP

- ESOP organizations could be set up by employees of a state-owned company registered in Hungary only for the purpose of purchasing a share of the company in which they were employees. Participation in an ESOP organization is the right of any employee employed for at least six months in a given company. According to the law, it is clear that membership in an ESOP organization is linked to employment, which means that the termination of employment entails the termination of the right to participate.
- There are no restrictions in setting up an ESOP organization. The only condition is that at least 40 percent of company employees should participate on a voluntary basis. Before the establishment of an ESOP organization, a preparatory committee should be set up. The most important task of the committee is the compilation of the feasibility study containing all parameters of employee ownership acquisition, including the method of payment and resources.
- Usually, the offer of the employees is evaluated among the other bids submitted to the state asset management organization, unless no other

25

bids are submitted or if the earlier bidding process was unsuccessful. According to the prevailing state asset policy guidelines, ESOP offers should be preferred to those submitted by other bidders when the proposals are similar.

- The ESOP organization established is the realization of the employee buyout, no other activity being permitted. Consequently, the ESOP organization is to be wound up after the full repayment of the loans.
- The law states the preferences that can be granted to the ESOP organization and the rules of using its own resources. An important provision is that if the private resources exceed the minimum prescribed by law, the business share purchased against this excess sum can be sold on. Until the loans have been fully repaid, the members of the ESOP organization are not free to dispose of the assets purchased on credit or installments.
- The ESOP organization has an option to repurchase assets it has sold, in certain circumstances, but the business shareholding acquired must be managed independently. The existence of a repayment period serves to protect the creditors.
- One of the most important documents of the ESOP organization is the Statutes, containing all major issues relating to the functioning of the organization, also taking into account the provisions of the law.

ESOP in Figures

In 1993, state asset sales through the ESOP increased in a spectacular manner. While in 1992 there were only 7 cases when employees bought up business shares, by the end of 1993 this number had reached 126, amounting to 23 billion forints. The number of new shareholders was 45,000. By the end of 1994, the total number of state-owned companies bought out through the ESOP was 195, with a total registered capital of 75.9 billion forints. The sales volume amounted to 56.9 billion forints, which means that ESOP organization paid on average 75 percent of book value (as opposed to other privatization transactions, where the average was only 65 percent). Privatization through the ESOP constituted 14 percent of all transactions, of which ESOP buyouts amounted to 38.5 billion forints. The proportion of companies privatized through ESOP reached 20 percent of the total. Companies privatized through the ESOP were mostly small in size, being predominantly in the processing industry and in trade, partially in the service and construction industries. The average proportion of company employees participating in the program was 68 percent.

Table 6

Number of ESOP Transactions
(Cumulative)

Year	Total ESOP (no.)	Majority ESOP (no.)
2d quarter 1992	1	1
3d quarter 1992	3	2
4th quarter 1992	7	4
1st quarter 1993	38	29
2d quarter 1993	59	45
3d quarter 1993	77	60
4th quarter 1993	126	87
4th quarter 1994	195	N/A

Source: SPA.

It is notable that almost 70 percent of ESOP transactions involved the acquisition of a majority holding in the company.

Table 7

Number of ESOP Buyouts
(Cumulative, Million Forints)

Year	Total ESOP	Majority ESOP
2d quarter 1992	655	655
3d quarter 1992	1,290	1,270
4th quarter 1992	1,744	1,566
1st quarter 1993	7,103	6,811
2d quarter 1993	13,566	12,655
3d quarter 1993	16,580	15,352
4th quarter 1993	23,776	20,776
4th quarter 1994	38,290	N/A

Source: SPA.

27

The dominance of ESOP organizations was very important, while—in spite of the expectations—the share of outside investors was negligible.

Table 8

Distribution of Companies Purchased by ESOP Organizations According to the Size of Registered Capital (until the End of 1993)

Limited liability companies million forints	Dec. 1993 No.	Dec. 1994 No.
0-10	3	5
10.1-50	16	23
50.1-100	13	14
100.1-200	11	16
200.1-500	10	12
500.1-1000	2	4
Joint-stock companies: million forints	No.	No.
0-10	7	7
10.1-50	35	35
50.1-100	15	15
100.1-200	5	16
200.1-500	3	36
500.1-1000	-	26
Above 1000	-	18

Source: SPA.

The distribution of companies owned by ESOP organizations according to size is relatively uniform. It should be noted that in 1994 most of the companies sold to ESOP organizations had registered capital exceeding 200 million forints.

While until the end of 1993 most of the companies sold to ESOP organizations had registered capital below 500 million forints (except in two cases), by the end of 1994 there were forty eight such companies. Of these, the registered capital of eighteen companies exceeded 1 billion forints (e.g., Centrum with 5 billion forints, MMG and Mogürt with 2.8 billion forints each, Masped with 2.6 billion forints, and Caola with 1.8 billion forints).

Table 9

Distribution of Companies Purchased by ESOP Organizations According to the Number of Employees (until the End of 1993)

Number of employees	Number of companies
0-50	13
51-100	20
101-200	22
201-300	15
301-500	21
501-1000	19
Above 1001	10

Source: SPA.

The figures show that during the 1993–94 period there was a real breakthrough in the ESOP program, which was mentioned earlier as a near-failure. In the beginning, companies privatized through the ESOP had quite small capital and the success of their operation mostly depended on the skills and the outside relationships of employees. But in 1994 ESOP organizations began to be set up with really large companies (e.g., Centrum). As mentioned previously, it is notable that most ESOP transactions involved the acquisition of a majority shareholding in the target company.

One limitation of the ESOP was the inevitable absence of additional capital, which narrowed the range of companies that could be privatized in this way. Most ESOP transactions could be characterized by the fact that additional capital was not an indispensable requirement. In practice, the ESOP was usually the last step when other forms of privatization had proved unsuccessful. The ESOP had the advantage of the shortness of time needed for its execution, which helped the acceleration of privatization.

In most of the cases, the main difficulty was the large uncertainty factor of the business plan, which constituted the basis of the feasibility study. The feasibility study had the task of proving that in each year during the term of the loan sufficient cashflow would be generated by the company to repay principal and interest, to pay a 20 percent profits tax, and to pay a dividend from after-tax profits. The difficulty lay in the impossibility of planning in a period of fast-changing markets and an uncertain economic outlook. Another risk was generated by the fact that most employees wanted to rescue their jobs by means of the ESOP initiative, which of itself could not guarantee anything.

One feature of most ESOP transactions was initiation (and never opposition) by management and serving as the background of a management buyout (MBO). A special case of the ESOP initiative was when a separate plant or independent unit wanted to secede from the parent company and used the ESOP as a tool to do so. In such cases, the business plan was especially difficult to prepare because the costs relating to the given plant or unit were not absolutely clear and some of the costs had been hidden as the overhead of the parent company.

In many cases, the ESOP sale served as a background for other transactions for an interim period while the foreign or domestic investors played for time until they could legitimize their steps with the ESOP. The question was how their future intentions and business opportunities could be matched by the survival of the ESOP in the long run.

The risk of ESOP sales will only be clear after the three-year grace period, when repayment becomes due and the viability of the whole construction can be assessed. It is an illusion, however, that companies privatized for cash start from a much better financial position than those privatized through the ESOP, because most investors—even if paying cash—financed the purchase price from bank loans. Thus the owner must pay principal and dividend from the returns of the privatized business also in this case.

In general, one should only talk about the failure of the ESOP construction if it can be safely assumed that more companies privatized through ESOP go bankrupt than those privatized otherwise. Experiences gathered so far do not support such an assumption.

After the enactment of the new Privatization Act in 1995 this program was also discontinued.

6.3. MBO

MBO is a privatization technique not covered by a separate law. Today the main feature of MBO is its concealment within the ESOP, using the preferences, not being averse to the use of personal assets either as investments or as collateral for bank loans. The business share to be purchased is used more and more as the collateral for an E-loan. In this case, the debt service is accounted for as company cost, meaning capital withdrawal from the company.

MBO is usually linked with the ESOP, partly in order to gain access to preferences, partly because in such a situation the keeping of the employees could serve as a basis for the managers' keeping their positions. It is very hard to conceptually separate MBO from ESOP, since, according to estimates, most ESOP transactions were simply MBOs by another name.

Different MBO techniques became prevalent, such as the straightforward manager buyout of the capital assets of the business, manager contracts, installment payments. E-loans, the ESOP, and the leasing systems. The acquisition of ownership by "celebrity" employees, who determine the company image, is also a type of MBO.

According to professional estimates, until the summer of 1993 almost half of all self-privatized companies—meaning 100 small and medium-sized companies—became controlled by their managers, amounting to 36 percent of the purchase price collected by the SPA. If we accept these data, practically all ESOP buyouts can be regarded as MBOs.

The Main Features of MBO

Buyouts resulting in exclusive employee (management) ownership, without the participation of external investors, used the ESOP in each case. Managers became the majority shareholders, and in other cases their shares in excess of 25 percent ensured that they had veto rights. The purchase price was mostly below 100 percent of book value, with no special relationship to the size of the company or the date of the purchase.

Due to the lack of in-depth knowledge about the companies, the SPA usually could not check the reality of the business plans in detail. This "weakness" was counterbalanced by its demand for a competitive bidding process and its acceptance of the business plan evaluation of the lender bank, without questioning the bank's commitments. In certain cases, the SPA could be convinced of the risk of a hostile takeover and a closed biding process was announced, although, to a certain extent, the information monopoly of managers helped in keeping out competitive bidders.

A relatively strong propaganda campaign was launched within the companies, attracting 70 to 80 percent of employees to participate in the acquisition. Nonetheless, the internal ownership proportions changed to the benefit of managers due to the score system set up in many companies to determine the number of shares that could be purchased by each employee. The score system was based on job, years of employment in the company, and salary, which resulted in very high scores for management. In other companies, no rules were set up to determine the number of shares that could be purchased by each employee. Here the main criterion was the individual contribution, which resulted in the dominance of managers who had more disposable savings to buy shares. An employee's contribution was usually HUF 20–50,000, while that of managers was HUF 100–700,000. The company frequently helped employees by paying extra salary or a bonus or even granting a loan guarantee.

Mostly managers got seats on the bodies representing the shareholders or the leadership of the ESOP organization. The managers of the companies reviewed almost never complained about the clumsy decision-making process due to the large number of shareholders. This fact indicates that the managers "buy out" not only the company but also their own jobs. This fact also has a negative side: lacking control, management is not ready to budge and the necessary replacements are not always made.

The banks usually demanded collateral security, typically to 150 percent of the loan granted. The lender banks usually insisted on being the debtor's account-keeping bank.

An interesting contradiction should be noted here. While in the West venture capital companies play an important role in MBO, in Hungary commercial banks are forced to fulfill that role even if they have a much different function. It is very understandable if the banks try to disperse the risk and favor those ESOP organizations where managers are in a majority, because this—in the banks' opinion—indicates the managers' commitment. Since 1995 MBO has been practically discontinued.

6.4. The Application of the Leasing Technique

For a long time the concept of MBO was not accepted politically. Then, in the autumn of 1992, the privatization leasing technique was introduced in order to involve managers in the privatization process. It was just an experiment and covered a relatively narrow area. The program targeted investors lacking cash but possessing sufficient personal assets that could serve as collateral for the loans granted.

The program had three protagonists: the SPA as lessor, the company to be leased, and the lessee. The Hungarian entrepreneur (the lessee) acquires ownership in the following manner:

- The lessee receives the business share in the form of a lease, enabling him to make the necessary business decisions.
- Due to the efficient management, the results of the company are expected to improve.
- The company pays a service fee to the lessee as a compensation for his management and organization services; this service fee finances the payment of the leasing fee.
- Upon the expiration of the leasing contract, the business share is transferred to the lessee.

The main elements of the leasing technique are as follows: The term of the leasing is six years, if below, and eight years, if above 100 million forints' leasing fee. The term is ten years in the agriculture, forestry, and food industries, independent of the leasing fee. The lessee pays the lease fee installments from the service fees received in exchange for his management-organization services rendered to the company. The service fee is regulated by a management-organization contract concluded simultaneously with the execution of the leasing contract between the company and the lessee. The extent and maturity of the service fee and the leasing fee are the same. The company transfers the fee it has received directly to the SPA.

During the term of the contract, the service fee can be reduced if its payment would reduce the assets of the company to such an extent that it could lead to the termination of the contract. In this case, the lessee must make up the difference between the two fees from his own resources. On the other hand, the service fee can be increased—when the company profits allow such an increase—thus enabling the lessee to pay the leasing fees faster, thereby shortening the term of the leasing contract. Such accelerated acquisition of property can also be financed from an external source. For this compensation certificates may also be used. At the time of the redemption of the certificates interest is added to their nominal value. The lease fees are indexed in the same way as the actual interest rate of E-loans.

As there is no grace period with the leasing technique, in order to counterbalance the initial burdens the first annual leasing fee installment is only 50 percent of the installments to be paid in later years. One condition of the bid is the availability of collateral worth at least the first annual leasing fee. As collateral the SPA accepts cash, compensation certificates, bank guarantees, foreign exchange deposits, securities, gold, and other artifacts or surety. The company itself cannot serve as collateral. Still, the preceding collateral mix could be very favorable, not only because of the flexibility of its possible composition, but also due to its relatively low cost, at least compared with other privatization techniques.

The lessee must further promise that, at the end of the term, the book equity of the company will be at least as high as it was at the time of contract execution. Even if it should fall, temporarily, lower than that, the difference might not exceed three times the collateral security.

One important element of the preferences hidden in the construction is the very attractive tax preference linked to privatization leasing. From a company tax aspect, the management-organization service fee rendered in case of privatization is considered as company cost, which can be charged to company results. Personal income tax must be paid on the purchase price (or at least the nominal value), but only if the business share is sold. The tax, if any, can be reduced by the amount of the leasing fee paid from own resources. The tax rate is the same as the withholding tax rate. As to general sales tax, the law mentioned before provides that no tax should be paid on these services or the leasing fee to be paid to the SPA.

The statistics of the first round are as follows: The total assets of the companies privatized in the first round were 3,678 million forints, of which 2,821 million forints were registered capital and 857 million forints were capital reserves. The registered capital of the companies was between 30 million forints and 850 million forints. The average proportion of reserves to registered capital was approximately 30 percent. The SPA share offered was 2,276 million forints, making up 80.6 percent of the total registered capital. In the 1990–92 period, total sales of the companies shrank by 32 percent, while total before tax profits (amounting to 112.4 million forints) changed to a loss (in 1992 total loss amounted to 68 million forints). In 1992 three companies were profitable, one just broke even, and four made losses. The companies meet the criteria of inefficient businesses badly in need of reorganization.

A total of sixteen bids were submitted to purchase the eight companies. One intended to pay in cash; all others wanted to avail of the leasing construction. Of the fifteen leasing bids, individuals submitted four and leasing groups eleven. The employees/managers of the companies submitted eight bids. (One general manager wanted to buy his own company.) The owners of companies being in business contact with or performing the same activity as the company to be purchased submitted six bids, and an outsider company submitted one bid. The eleven leasing groups had memberships between two and thirteen and an average membership of five or six, which is the optimal number for efficient decision making. Within the groups, the ownership expectancy distribution was equal in four cases, dominant (one member being above 50 percent) in five cases, and unequal without domination in two cases.

The highest leasing bids offered 95 percent of book value, while the average of the total was 79 percent and the average of the six known winning bids was 73.9 percent. Collateral was mostly real estate (in 33 percent of the cases); in the rest of the cases it was invested assets (32 percent),

Table 10

Leasing Sales in the 1991-94 period

	1991	*1992*	*1993*	*1994*	*Total*
Quantity	-	-	9.00	15.00	24.00
Nominal value (billion forints)	-	-	2.99	3.10	6.09

Source: SPA.

bank deposits (13 percent), or bank guarantees (22 percent).

The main features of the average leased company were the following:

- The company was of relatively small size and geographically concentrated, which meant that the collateral was not very high and the company was more transparent.
- The company profile was services, so the requirement to renew technology was not as important as in the case of manufacturing.
- The conditions for fast asset restructuring were in place, thus improving efficiency and the liquidity position. (Indebtedness here played no role; even indebted companies could be leased, as the company could not serve as collateral anyway. By means of asset restructuring the debt burden can be reduced).
- When transforming the company the capital structure was formulated in

35

such a manner that the proportion of registered capital and reserve capital should be in line with the company positions.

- The company management had clear-cut turnaround programs and ideas, even if these carried risks.
- The company was of linear organizational structure, the responsibility and decision-making paths were clear and simple, and the data could be easily focused for the managers guiding the turnaround program—which was of special importance at the beginning of the program. This meant that in this respect those companies were considered better that formulated their new structure only after the execution of and by taking into account the leasing contract.

Of course, the leasing technique could also be used for companies whose parameters are less ideal than those outlined here, but in that case the speed and success of reorganization could suffer.

Leasing was a typical MBO technique. After 1995 the new act also brought this program to an end.

3

Capital Loss in the State Sector and the Reasons

1. Gradual Elimination of Subsidies

The 1968 reform replaced direct (administrative) control over state enterprises with indirect control through financial means, which resulted—in addition to a series of negative consequences—in a basically positive change. Mainly thanks to this, the Hungarian economy became more efficient, within the defined framework of Communism, than the other Communist economies. In addition, a generation of economists came of age becoming committed to economic reforms. As to state-owned enterprises, the financial (profitability) aspect gradually gained ground. State control—including continuous financial meddling, subsidies, and tax holidays—made economic transparency, however, almost impossible. Therefore, the demand to do away with tax holidays and labeled subsidies could be deemed absolutely positive.

Simultaneously with the justified abolition of subsidies the tax burden of industrial enterprises should have been reduced at least accordingly. This was the time when the first error was committed (by the government, the opposition, and the international financial bodies, first of all the IMF). They wanted to transform the Hungarian economy—and, within it, Hungarian large-scale industry—in an environment of financial restrictions. Precisely when more resources were needed a series of measures were introduced to reduce the available resources drastically. Nobody could expect socialist industry to be transformed in line with the altered and basically more strict market requirements in an environment where much fewer resources were available than earlier. In fact the situation was worse, because the financial positions and technical levels of enterprises deteriorated at an accelerated pace. In the former East Germany it was axiomatic that industrial restructuring needed huge additional resources. However, in

37

the other ex-COMECON countries economic transition was accompanied by the drastic reduction of resources, and Hungary was again the leader of the pack. This is how the policy of using up the assets was begun. As a consequence of this policy, assets worth hundreds of billions of forints have been lost during the past seven years.

2. The Administrative Suspension of Exports to the East

The using up of assets and resources was significantly accelerated by the suspension of exports to the Soviet Union. The collapse of Eastern markets was to a large extent the result of political intervention, occurring with the consent of the government and the opposition. Noting that the Soviet partner was unable to pay for Hungarian exports (in kind or in hard currency), exports were suspended. Before making that decision, however, we should have considered the consequences. What would exporters do if they lost their market? It was clear that most idle capacities could not be used for anything else, as the domestic demand shrank due to the restrictive policies of the government, while only a fraction of these exports could be sold to the West. What was the profitability of Soviet exports and how much could be saved by their suspension? Arguably, exports were so profitable that they could have remained affordable even if only a third of the sales price had been paid. On the other hand, the enterprises had overhead costs even if production lines remained idle. Furthermore, most profits from Eastern exports were reaped by suppliers of parts and not by the manufacturers of the final products.

How much state revenue was lost due to the suspension of Eastern exports? It was not customary to consider the negative effect of a slump in the economy on the state budget. Experts only focused on the elimination of losses, without calculating taxes and contributions not paid to the state budget by the manufacturer and its suppliers. What was the percentage of exports that would not have been paid? Two factors should not have been forgotten. First, some Soviet imports from Hungary were replaced by hard-currency imports. Second, the greater the Soviet partner's debt, the greater the willingness would have been to export world-marketable products to Hungary. What the behavior of the West would have been to Hungary with several billion forints owed by Russia is now clear. Hungary could have received much more Western aid, indirectly as well as directly.

How much is an active Hungarian presence in the markets of the former Soviet Union worth in the international capital market? We should have realized in the course of privatization that foreign capital was interested in Hungary mainly because of its involvement in the Eastern markets. The moment this involvement stopped in the industrial sector, the most important from the aspect of privatization, interest shrank to a fraction of its earlier size. Once Eastern exports were suspended, the market value of such giants as Richter Pharmaceuticals and Ikarus Bus became almost negligible in the eyes of Western investors. Nonpaid exports could have been counterbalanced merely by the capital loss caused by the suspension of Eastern exports.

3. The Tax Levied on Fictive Profits Caused by Inflation

The using up of company assets started to accelerate when the inflation rate ran into double digits. Even in the presence of a modern accounting law, the tax makes disclosure of real profits practically impossible. The higher the inflation rate, the bigger the inflation loss disclosed as national product and fictive profit, which in turn is heavily taxed. Although the practice made economic transparency impossible, it was still maintained in a high-inflation environment, because it legalized the using up of assets by the government and simultaneously meant significant tax revenues. Luckily, this state budget revenue generated by fictive company profits has melted to such an extent that maybe now it will be possible to prepare realistic balance sheets.

The practice of disclosing asset price inflation as company profit is widespread in the West. It is necessary in order to prevent tampering with company profits for the sake of tax evasion. In the West, however, the inflation rate rarely exceeds 10 percent and, in any event, the effects are set off by higher rates of depreciation. In justified cases, asset revaluation is possible everywhere and the resulting fictive asset growth is tax-free. In the West, fictive company profits caused by inflation do not result in a withdrawal of assets. On the contrary, in practice a significant part of real company asset growth will not be taxed at all, due to accelerated depreciation.

In a high-inflation environment, if no revaluation occurs the withdrawal of company assets through taxation gets accelerated. In this case, the real value of depreciation gets reduced in line with the inflation rate and the reduction is taxed as profits. If the depreciation rate is 10 percent and the inflation rate 20 percent, 2 percent of asset value appears as fictive profits, which is—in the case of a 50 percent profit tax—nothing less than a capital tax of 1 percent levied on the gross asset value. (Note that if the average net asset of companies is 50 percent of gross value, the capital tax rate levied on the operating assets is already 2 percent. This is not dramatic in a single year but intolerable over a longer period.) The depreciation rate projected to the asset value adjusted to real price was 1.3 percent in 1993, as opposed to the minimum justified rate of 8 percent (4 percent in 1980 and 2 percent in 1988). The minimum amortization is 8 percent in the West, and this would be roughly the depreciation rate in Hungary if during asset valuation the inflationary distortions were screened out.

In 1988 half of amortization justified on the basis of depreciation rates could still be disclosed as cost. In 1992 prices, the fictive national product and actual using up of assets disclosed this way only amounted to 63 billion forints, whereas in 1993 only 30 percent of the normative amortization could be accounted for and the fictive national product and actual using up of state assets disclosed was 206 billion forints. This means that two-thirds of amortization costs—being low anyway—were disclosed as before-tax profits. In that year the annual capital tax rate on gross value was nearly 3 percent, corresponding to a rate of 6 percent on net value. Even in the West, such a tax rate would be intolerable. Let us assume that in a given Western country the profit rate on net asset value is 6 percent and the assets are amortized at 50 percent. If we use our system in such an environment, real company profits would be zero, meaning zero market value for company assets, which is determined by the actual capitalized profits of the company, i.e., the real asset growth of the owner. Therefore, the fact must be accepted that in an environment where inflation is rampant and the known accounting standards are in place within a few years' time the market value of companies to be privatized has disappeared.

4. Transformation Using the Wrong Asset Approach

The transformation law called for asset revaluation but interpreted transformation to mean the sale of assets at current market value. This corresponds to the purchase of a four-year-old car for one-fifth of the new car price. The car can then be depreciated according to the prevailing rate. The method is absolutely correct in cases of insignificant values compared with the asset value of the company, but even if something is insignificant, it could be illogical without causing any trouble. However, it was a big mistake to follow this practice during the transformation of state-owned companies.

What does the amortization of the market price of assets depreciated in this way mean? The basic reduction of justified amortization. Still using the preceding example, a car can be depreciated in five years; i.e. the annual amortization is one-fifth of the new car price, so the first year's amortization after resale should be the purchase price and not one-fifth of it.

In the transformation system introduced, amortization could only be calculated on the net value at the time of transformation. The net asset value of the top 500 U.S. companies is roughly 60 percent of market capitalization. If their legal form should be transformed and this legal act would acknowledge only a value depreciated to 60 percent, the amount of the present 10 percent amortization would be reduced in one moment to 60 percent of the original, and profit tax would be payable on the difference.

5. The Application of the Bankruptcy Law

In Hungarian practice, the operation of loss-making companies is deemed harmful. The concept was correct in the last century and remains so if two conditions are met: the weight of contributions demanded by the state is relatively low, and the capital and labor becoming redundant at the company can be used more efficiently elsewhere. In Hungary, the first condition cannot be met, because the state levies heavy taxes on industry even when compared with the West. But payments to the state budget (including social security contributions) are costs only at the company level. At the level of society as a whole, they are sources of revenue. On this basis, a company is useful to society if it makes a lower loss than the sum of taxes, contributions, and duties it pays to the state. During the last ten years, hardly any company made a loss in this sense. The balance of the state budget deteriorates if a company duly paying its taxes is laid idle.

The situation is different in the case of the second condition, i.e., when the loss-making company is laid idle because the capital and labor becoming redundant could be used more efficiently elsewhere. In this case, however, even a profitable company could be laid idle, so long as capital and labor could be diverted for a more profitable use. Unfortunately, this is not the case in Hungary. After a company is laid idle, its working force just joins the mass of unemployed people, while the bulk of its capital gets definitely lost. It follows that no company should be laid idle unless its losses are bigger than the total revenue it generates for the state budget and 80 percent of wage costs equal the sum of the whole of amortization. (Eight percent of wage costs must be taken into account because this is roughly the cost of paying unemployment benefits.)

In the majority of cases, however, even these companies should be kept alive. If we take into consideration the future prospects of losses being reduced and the loss of professional skills of the working force, the case is stronger. Furthermore, the social tensions caused by a high rate of unemployment could be critical in Hungary, because in the past decades unemployment was unknown and job security is valued very highly by the bulk of society.

6. The Unprecedented Interest Rate Margin

Asset withdrawal due to the reasons outlined previously shrank the resources of industry, already heavily in debt. Then an interest system was introduced by which an interest margin unprecedented in economic history became inevitable. The joint effects of the interest tax collected on deposits, the large central bank deposit obligation, the reduction of production brought about by government means, and the shortage of company resources resulted in an almost unprecedented credit risk. As a consequence, the loan interest rate payable by companies became almost 20 percent higher than the bank deposit rate. While the latter was roughly the same as the inflation rate, making the real deposit interest rate equal to 0 percent, companies were forced to pay a real interest on their borrowings that was hitherto unknown in Hungarian economic history.

At the same time that companies had a negative profit on their operating capital they had to pay a real interest rate of 10 to 20 percent on their loans. As a consequence, companies were sucked dry by the banks, which became hugely profitable. The bank profits were partly spent, partly paid into the state budget as tax and dividends. This source dried up as companies were bankrupted by the outrageous loan rates, in turn bankrupting their lender banks. The number of bad loans skyrocketed, and more and more companies stopped payments altogether, prompting the legislation on debtor, bank, and credit consolidation.

7. Capital Loss in Figures

Although accounting law declares principles of truth and accuracy, it forces companies operating in a high-inflation environment to prepare balance sheets and profit and loss accounts that contradict those principles. Due to inflation rates that turned double-digit in 1991 and accounting standards introduced by a state that decided to ignore the hard facts, the entries of synthetic company accounts became more and more untrue.

Although the amendment of the accounting law at the beginning of 1995 allowed the revaluation of net asset value under certain circumstances, the adjustment of gross asset value and amortization were forbidden. As far as the draft wording of the new amendment is known, this situation will not be changed. For the sake of this study, adjusted value is understood as the purchase price (or value) of the past expressed by the monetary value of a later period (the reverse of value adjustment with unchanged prices).

Which is better: the current, the unchanged, or the adjusted price? The question is unanswerable for a long time frame. Each price is good or bad, true or fictive, depending on the accounting objectives. From the aspect of replacement, the adjusted price is the true price, whereas the original procurement price is a fictive price.

The big advantage of adjustment is that data calculated at today's prices are much more informative than those calculated at historical prices. Today's prices are felt directly, and thus the data can be observed on a practical scale. Younger people, in particular, could be hard put to handle prices that prevailed before they were born.

Another advantage of adjustment is its compatibility with current-price accounting and thus with current-price statistical data as well. With the advanced information technology of today, the additional cost of calculations and other steps needed for adjustment are dwarfed by the advantages offered by this tool.

For the sake of addition and subtraction it is essential that all costs and returns should be expressed in monetary values of the same year, because in theory only values discounted or adjusted to the same year should be associated. In the period studied, there could be fourfold to twentyfold differences between the forint values of different years. These should not be added without adjustment, as apples are not added to pears or (without conversion) dollars to forints. The same should be noted when summing time series.

Amortization for machinery, equipment, and vehicles could be for periods of a few years or for ten to twenty years, and amortization for real estate and buildings could be for even a hundred years. Thus in the course of analysis the adjustment period can be quite long.

The twenty-one year period of 1976–1997 is suitable for the review of replacement problems of machinery, equipment, and vehicles having amortization rates of 5 percent per annum. Buildings had to be handled as a special case, and we had to reach back to a period as early as the 1950s.

7.1. The Shrinking and Relative Shortage of Investments

The presenting of macroeconomic data starts with the review of investment data and price indices. The adjustment (price) factors necessary for the adjustment of asset and amortization values to the 1996 price level can be deducted from the investment price indices.

Adjustment is of fundamental importance, since the bulk of company bookkeeping and accounting in Hungary is carried out at current prices. Very little data among the accounting entries are recorded at historical value, apart from certain asset values and amortization costs deducted.

Table 11 shows the analysis results relating to the last eight years in the very long-range time series (going back to 1950) at current and 1996 prices. Figure 1 shows the most important relations of the long-term changes of investments.

As to the concept of investment shortage, the principal question concerns the comparison. In what sense is there a shortage? A stagnating investment level could be taken as a basis or a linear growth characteristic of healthy economies. The most important basis for comparison is, however, the real replacement need.

As to stagnation, the year to be taken as a basis is also important. The largest relative investment shortage is shown if we take the peak year of investments, 1979, as a basis.

In this example, the investment shortage is 6,048 billion forints in the

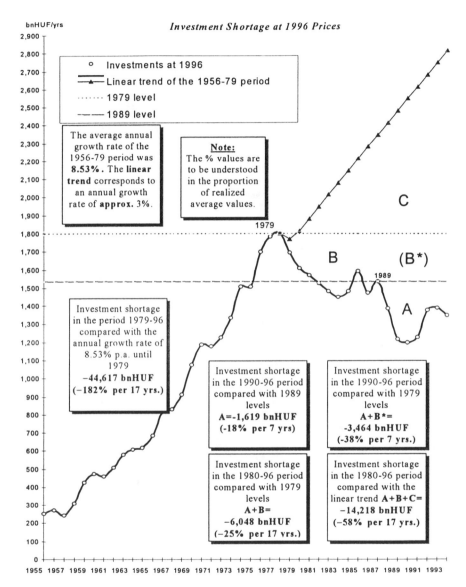

Figure 1

Table 11

Gross and Net Investment Surpluses and Shortages during the Transition Period in Hungary											
Item	No.	Source or formula	Unit	1989	1990	1991	1992	1993	1994	1995	1996
Gross investment data											
Investment at current prices	1	NBS	bnHUF p.a.	340	356	492	556	638	843	1.120	1.347
Volume index for previous year	2	NBS	1 / year	1.044	0.902	0.887	0.984	1.024	1.123	1.010	0.970
Adjustment (price) factors for 1996	3	Own calculation	1 / × year	4.522	3.887	2.469	2.152	1.918	1.632	1.240	1.000
Investment at 1996 prices	4	Rows 1*3	bnHUF p.a.	1,536	1,385	1,215	1,195	1,224	1,375	1,389	1,347
Investment shortage compared with 1989 levels											
Annual shortage	5	Row 4.	bnHUF p.a.	0	−151	−321	−340	−311	−160	−147	−188
Cumulated shortage	6	Row 5.	bnHUF p.a.	0	−151	−472	−812	−1,123	−1,284	−1,431	−1,619
Cumulated shortage compared with actual investments	7	Rows 4. and 6.	(%)	0	−10.9	−18.2	−21.4	−22.4	−20.1	−18.4	−17.7
Adjusted (real) and book (monetary) annual depreciation and net investments											
Book (monetary) depreciation	8	Own estimates	bnHUF p.a.	583	506	420	593	602	564	496	438
Real adjusted depreciation (Real replacement needs)	9	Own estimates	bnHUF p.a.	1,254	1,196	1,131	1,481	1,418	1,380	1,286	1,242
Annual replacement needs at 1996 prices	10	8-9	bnHUF p.a.	−672	−689	−711	−888	−815	−816	−791	−804
Monetary net investment value	11	4-8	bnHUF p.a.	953	878	795	603	622	811	893	909
Real net investment value	12	4-9	bnHUF p.a.	282	189	84	−286	−194	−5	102	105
Real and monetary net investment in the period											
Proportion of monetary net investments	13	11/9	(%)	76.0	73.5	70.3	40.7	43.9	58.8	69.4	73.2
Proportion of real net investments	14	13/9	(%)	22.4	15.8	7.4	−19.3	−13.7	−0.3	8.0	8.5

Source: Privatization Research Institute.

1980–96 period, a huge figure. This figure is 2.6 percent greater than actual investment during this seventeen-year period. In other words, even in a stagnating environment, 25 percent more value would have been invested than actually took place.

According to these calculations, the Hungarian economy is chronically "underfed." The investment figures are national economy data, containing the investments of the private sphere, the state and municipality bodies, the foreign-owned business organizations, etc. In the same way as a protracted chronic illness causes loss of health, this causes general destruction in the organization of the economy. Investments are the driving force, the engine of the economy. If investment levels are chronically low, then this causes a deep recession in the long run. This is, in fact, the case in Hungary, and the data converted to 1996 prices point at this with dramatic force.

Investment shortage can also be compared to the last year of Communism, 1989. If 1989 is taken as the basis, the investment shortage was 1,619 billion forints in the 1990–96 period, which results in a ratio of 18 percent to actual investment during this seven-year period.

We also reviewed actual investments compared to linear growth and illustrated it in a curve starting from 1979. The graph shows the investment shortage in a spectacular manner. It should be noted that in the given quantitative position this linear trend corresponds to an annual growth rate of nearly 3 percent.

In the 1979–95 period, investment shortage compared to linear growth was 14,218 billion forints. This produces a ratio of 58 percent of actual investment during this seventeen-year period.

These data are cautious preliminary estimates. Taking the most recent preliminary data issued by the information service of the Central Bureau of Statistics as a basis, instead of the CBS volume published in September 1996, the investment shortage would have been even bigger, due to the major drop in investments in 1995 (ignored here). For instance, taking 1989 as a basis, the result would have been 1,860 billion forints in the 1990–96 period, and taking 1979 as a basis, the result would have been 6,535 billion forints in the 1980–96 period.

In the 1956–79 period, investment growth came closer to the exponential trend belonging to the annual growth rate of 8.5 percent than to the linear trend. Once we compare investment shortage to this growth rate, the figure in the 1979–95 period is 44,617 billion forints. This indicates a shortfall of 182 percent of actual investment during this seventeen-year period.

7.2. The Investment Shortage Compared to the Replacement Needs

The investment shortage figures shown previously do not reveal whether there are net investments above the real replacement needs. By definition, net investments are the sum of gross investments minus amortization. In the beginning of the 1990s, the CBS stopped calculating net investments due to the falsely synthesized accounting data. Lacking amortization calculation, the CBS was unable to publish net results, net investments, and other net parameters on a national economy level. Thus the present calculations fill a gap and lead to a number of results that cannot be found in Hungarian statistics or the economic literature. Some results may be questionable, but not their magnitude, at least not until the CBS experts start to calculate the net parameters.

For the CBS, however, to report statistics for the past is much more difficult than for it to reveal the present or forecast the future. It is possible to gather data in the present period or for the future, but it is virtually impossible to do so relating to the past. Thus in Hungary capitalist society is reintroduced without capital statistics, blindfolded, as it were. There are discussions about capital, capital loss, and privatization, but without real knowledge on the size of national assets and capital operating in Hungary, net investments, net domestic product, or the net values of profit and income.

Figure 2 illustrates, and the lower part of table 11 shows, the time series of real net investments. Net investments can be had as gross investments minus amortization. Amortization, however, can be calculated as book value (fictive) amortization and adjusted (real) amortization. If real amortization (equaling real replacement needs) is subtracted from gross investments, the value of real investments is received, while if fictive amortization is subtracted from gross investments, the result will be the value of fictive net investments.

In the 1956–65 period, real net investments were negative, because gross investments lagged behind real replacement needs. According to my calculations, the net investment shortage amounted to approximately 1,361 billion forints in this ten-year period.

In the 1966—91 period, however, gross investments exceeded real re-

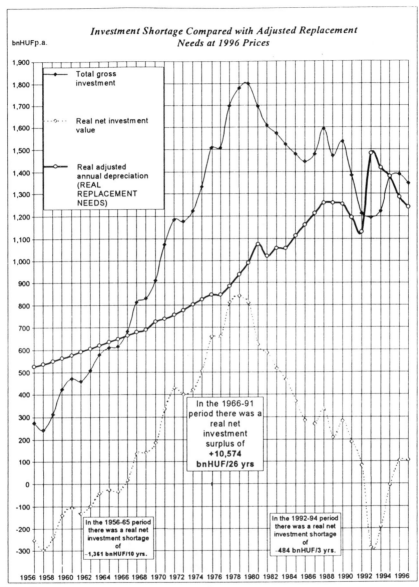

Figure 2

placement needs. In the 26 years of this period, net investments amounted to approximately 10,574 billion Forints. This expansion occurred in spite of a replacement shortage, a feature of the whole 1956–96 period, shown by the table and illustrated by the figure. But the two facts do not contradict each other. The results show that in the 1956–95 period sources of replacements were not—or not only—amortization but diverse other sources as well.

In theory, replacements should be financed from amortization and net investments should be financed from profits or outside capital as the following block diagram below.

In practice, a significant part of amortization was not allowed to accumulate, and the remaining part was heavily taxed or withdrawn from the enterprises in other ways.

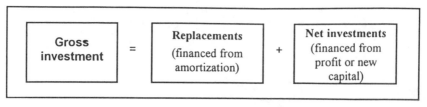

When amortization was less than real replacement needs, the book values of the enterprise were increased. As enterprises also used these partly fictive results for investments, an enterprise could have net investments and replacement shortage simultaneously, even without the use of outside capital.

Based on the centralized amortization funds, the state performed significant investment activities, partly by subsidizing company investments, partly by initiating large-scale state investments. The time series shown indicates this activity as well, also including the construction of family houses performed by the family itself as imputed by the CBS.

In the 1992–94 period, net investment became negative partly because the state quite abruptly restrained its own investments and the investment subsidies granted to enterprises. The number of family houses built was also reduced. This was the period when a majority of enterprises went bankrupt or went into liquidation. On a national economic level this reduced the volume of investments.

In the 1995–96 period, net investments became positive again. It can be assumed that the reason was partly the restart of economic growth, partly the increase of foreign investments in the form of physical capital.

7.3. Reduction of Asset Values

After the analysis of investment data, we continued with the analysis of material asset data (adjusting the asset data to the monetary value of the given year using adjustment factors and converting all data to the monetary values of 1996.)

Adjustment to the monetary value of the given year—e.g., 1990—makes sense because in this way current-price data can be had that is compatible with the current annual accounting data. The objective of adjustment to 1996 is to bring data of different periods to a common and comparable form.

During the adjustment process, we met a very serious calculation problem, namely, the sixty-to-eighty-year amortization cycle of real estate. Adjustment means that the procurement value must be multiplied by the price increase indices of the period from procurement until the year reviewed.

If the review starts in 1996, this means that we should go back to the beginning of the century, unless revaluation occurred in between. It can be assumed, however, that after the Second World War—during reconstruction and after the introduction of the new currency—real properties were recorded more or less at the monetary value of that date. Since then, eventual differences have been screened out from the time series by amortization. Consequently, it seems safe to calculate asset values and adjustments only in the 1950–96 period, continuously monitoring the annual movements of fixed assets, including the price changes.

Another basic problem had to be overcome in the course of the preparation of the estimates. At the beginning of the 1990s, the CBS corrected fixed asset values retroactively, even for the years before 1988. This study also used these corrected data (relying on, in addition to the data of the 1980–91 period, data relating to 1970 and 1980, prepared by the CBS).

Up to 1988, the adjustment process consisted of adding the adjusted value of the previous year to the annual increment of current-price book value (as the current-price increment is not to be adjusted for the given year). In addition, a correction deduction factor was used, which was determined empirically. The reason for the use of this correction factor is explained by the fact that additional amortization should be disclosed after the gross value increased through adjustment. The increment would accelerate amortization and replacement in relation to the actual status. For the 1990–96 period this was the only basis to determine the adjusted value of material assets, because in a period of so much company transformation, bankruptcy, and liquidation the changes to the values of fixed assets (and, within that, machinery) were totally uncontrollable.

Due to the absence of CBS reviews, the basic statistical processing of these data cannot be performed for this period, even now. (CBS experts hold the same opinion.) Basic data cannot be gathered subsequently. (Even the legal successor companies are hard to find, not to mention missing bookkeeping data.) This is the reason that would require other researchers to use data supported by some kind of model or empirical matching in order to replace the missing data of this period.

As to the results of the empirical matching process, it is important to note that the resulting adjustment factors harmonized with the data relating to the eighteen companies analyzed later.

Table 12 summarizes the calculations relating to the 1989–96 period. The changes in the 1991–92 period resulted in a break in the trend in 1993. The results of the adjustment process show that the asset value of machinery has shrunk continuously since 1992, while that of real property has shrunk continuously since 1993. As total asset value is determined by the value of real property, the net value of total fixed assets also shows a decreasing tendency since 1993.

Figure 3 also shows that in the 1994–96 period net asset value—i.e. operating physical capital—was reduced by 2,198 billion forints according to the calculations. This amounted to 6.2 percent of the peak value of 1993.

The decrease was huge in absolute numbers but modest in percentage figures. The graph fails to illustrate this accurately, but the decrease of machinery within the total asset value can still be seen. In the 1994–96 period, the loss in value of machinery amounted to 945 billion forints. The calculations show that in these three years almost 7.3 percent of machinery assets were lost. According to the calculations, the value loss of real property amounted to almost 1,253 billion forints in the same period, corresponding to 1.4 percent of all real property.

These unusually large numbers are in reality not too big as far as proportions are concerned. Their magnitude is due to their being adjusted values relating to the end of 1996 and not the book value.

Adjustment to 1996 prices is not a simple book value—price factor multiplication. It is simultaneously a value correction relating to the given year (by an adjustment factor relating to the given year). This double multiplication is the reason why we get adjusted values that are three to four

Table 12

Gross and Net Value Amortization Replacement Needs and Shortage of Fixed Assets on National Economic Level											
Volume	No.	Source or formula	Unit	1989	1990	1991	1992	1993	1994	1995	1996
Gross book and adjusted value at current and 1996 prices and the gross adjustment factors											
Gross book value at adjusted current price	1	Based on	bnHUF	5,835	6,090	6,453	7,509	8,591	9,458	10,686	11,734
Gross book value at 1996 price	2	own	bnHUF	18,684	16,761	14,784	14,961	15,216	14,215	13,061	11,734
Gross adjusted value at 1996 price	3	calculations	bnHUF	45,750	45,568	44,926	44,273	43,604	42,976	42,402	41,886
Gross adjustment (price) factor for the given year	4	3/2	(-)	2.46	2.72	3.04	2.96	2.87	3.02	3.25	3.57
Net book and adjusted value at current and 1996 prices and the net adjustment factors											
Net book value at adjusted current price	5	Based on	bnHUF	4,052	4,321	4,772	5,778	6,869	7,491	8,383	9,117
Gross book value at 1996 price	6	own	bnHUF	12,962	11,882	10,943	11,513	12,165	11,253	10,245	9,117
Net adjusted value at 1996 price	7	calculations	bnHUF	32,221	32,639	33,498	34,068	35,096	34,359	33,591	32,898
Net adjustment (price) factor for the given year	8	7/6	(-)	2.49	2.75	3.06	2.96	2.88	3.05	3.28	3.61
Depreciation period, rate and annual value											
Depreciation rate	9	Own calculation	year	36.6	38.1	39.7	29.9	30.8	31.1	33.0	33.7
Depreciation period	10	100/9	% p. a.	2.73	2.62	2.52	3.35	3.25	3.21	3.03	2.97
Book depreciation at current price	11	Own	bnHUF	180	182	186	300	340	972	404	438
Book depreciation at 1996 price	12	calculation	bnHUF	583	506	420	593	602	564	496	438
REAL ANNUAL REPLACEMENT NEEDS AND SHORTAGE and depreciation adjustment factors											
Adjusted depreciation (real annual replacement needs) at 1996 price	13	13+14	BnHUF	1,254	1,196	1,131	1,481	1,418	1,380	1,286	1,242
real annual replacement shortage	14	13+14	bnHUF	−672	−689	−711	−888	−815	−816	−791	−804
Depreciation (price) factor for the given year	15	15/12	(-)	2.15	2.36	2.69	2.50	2.35	2.45	2.60	2.84

Source: Privatization Research Institute, 1996.

times the book value. If we make a rough estimate and divide the asset value adjusted to 1996 prices (approximately 32,900 billion forints) by four, the result will be an asset value of "only" 8,200 billion forints. This seems realistic, even to a reader accustomed to the magnitude of book values.

This total asset value includes the assets of companies, the private sphere, state administration, municipalities and nonprofit institutions, and

Figure 3

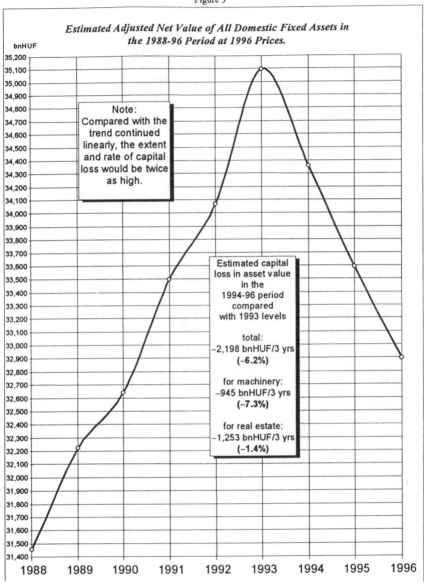

Estimated Adjusted Net Value of All Domestic Fixed Assets in the 1988-96 Period at 1996 Prices.

all movable or real property directly reviewed by the CBS. By implication, the figure includes household assets as well.

Regarding the asset values, the capital loss estimate was prepared only compared with the peak value of 1993. Capital loss could also have been calculated for the case of the linear or exponentially growing trend of the asset value being maintained after 1993. If compared with the linear trend, the capital loss would be doubled. The asset value trend for the long period starting with 1952 is not, however, of a linear but of an exponential nature. Consequently, the shortage of the recent years could also have been compared with the long-term growth trends.

Table 12 also shows the results of deduction of replacement needs and shortage. Amortization was calculated from the corrected book values divided by the amortization period. When the gross value is corrected, amortization will also show a corrected value.

The annual amortization adjusted to 1996 prices was calculated from the adjusted gross values divided by the amortization period. The annual replacement shortage was calculated as the difference between book amortization and adjusted amortization.

4

The Closing Phase and Evaluation of Privatization

In the period of spontaneous privatization (1987–90), the Treasury had no privatization revenue. In 1989 major foreign investments began (Hungaria Insurance, Tungsram), without any privatization revenue for the Treasury. In the 1990–94 period, most of privatization revenue was in the form of foreign currency. The state used these privatization revenues partly to replenish foreign exchange reserves, partly to finance the trade balance deficit. The bulk of privatization revenues in forints was used to finance the budget deficit. Apart from paying the direct and indirect costs of privatization, privatization revenues were not used to reduce foreign debt or for financing state investments. In 1995 the sale of the power sector and MATÁV gave the Treasury privatization revenue, which was almost as large as the entire privatization revenue of the 1990–94 period. This revenue was also a foreign currency. The government submitted to the Parliament a proposal relating to the use of the exceptionally high privatization revenue ($3 billion) of 1995. The Parliament approved the government proposal, and the bulk of the privatization revenue was used to reduce external debt. A part was used to finance the annual budget deficit, and a very small part was used to finance state investments. In 1996 the government basically spent privatization revenue to finance the budget deficit and company restructuring. In the finishing phase of privatization (1997–98) it is expected that the SPH will use the bulk of privatization revenue to meet state obligations relating to earlier privatization transactions. It seems that the privatization revenues of the 1990–94 period could have been spent more usefully on infrastructure and other investments instead of financing the budget deficit. In all probability, the huge privatization revenue of 1995 could have been spent more usefully on the development of the real economy, meaning especially infrastructure and midsized companies.

2. Important Privatization Transactions in the 1995–97 Period

2.1. Privatization of MOL

MOL is the national oil and gas company of Hungary. It is unique in central Eastern Europe because it is the only fully integrated oil and gas company in the region. In 1995 MOL was the largest company in Hungary, with gross sales of almost $U.S. 3 billion. MOL deals with oil processing and distribution, the wholesale and retail sale of oil products, oil and gas exploration, production, transport, and storage. In certain areas, the company has a monopoly; in others, it is the market leader in Hungary.

The new Privatization Act of 1995 provided for keeping the company permanently in state hands up to the extent of 25 percent of the shares + 1 share. Its privatization is a multiphase process, being executed through share offerings. Table 13 shows the ownership structure of the company in 1995, in the second phase of privatization.

Table 13

Ownership Structure of MOL in 1995

	Nominal value of stocks (million forints)	Share %
SPH	86,928	88.3
Municipalities and private investors	11,472	11.7
Total	98,400	100.0

Source: SPH.

The company held its general meeting on October 16, 1995, deciding to issue a single preference share assuring special rights (golden share) to be subscribed by the SPH. The golden share gives the representative of the state the right to veto certain decisions in order to protect national interest. (The most important of these is the decision relating to the sale of strategic assets.)

The first share offering was in 1995. As a result of the transaction, MOL common stock was listed on the BSE and global deposit certificates representing common stock were listed on the Luxembourg Stock Exchange and also by the PORTAL and SEAQ OTC systems. Table 14 shows the result of share offerings at the end of 1995.

Table 14
Share Offerings in MOL to End of 1995

	Nominal value of shares sold	
	(bnHUF)	(%)
Private allocation to foreign institutional investors	18.500	18.8
ESOP	5.272	5.4
MBO in cash installments	387	0.4
Public offering to domestic institutional and small-scale investors	3.197	3.2
Shares kept in reserve (oversubscription option)	1.903	1.9
Total	29.259	29.7

Source: SPH.

The company represented almost one-third of all BSE shares, and MOL share turnover is also one of the largest in the stock exchange. The initial public offering at the end of 1995 was the largest single sale on the Hungarian capital market. The size of the block of shares bought up by international investors is more than three times as large as that of the second-largest block of shares sold (that of the OTP Bank). The transaction exceeded $170 million, making it the largest public offering not only in Hungarian history but also in the region as a whole. (The second-largest transaction in the region took place in Poland, where a block of shares of a bank worth $148 million was sold.) The company ownership structure (following the second phase of privatization is shown in table 15).

In 1994 the municipalities still held 6.7 percent of the company. Later they partly sold their shares in the OTC market, and it was expected that the would sell off the rest in 1997–98. At the beginning of 1997, the SPH still held 58.6 percent of the company. The Privatization Act set a deadline of December 31, 1997, after which state ownership in the company must not exceed 25 percent of the shares + 1 share. In the 1997–2000 period, the 4.47 percent employee ownership is expected to decrease, while the 0.4 percent share the management is expected to increase. The reason is that in the 1997–2000 period MOL dividends are expected to be lower than those of other companies (in the chemical and pharmaceutical industry) listed on the BSE or of government securities. As opposed to MOL management,

58

Table 15

	Stock nominal value (million forints)	Share (%)
SPH	57.669	58.6
Municipalities	1.673	1.7
Foreign institutions	28.241	28.7
Own shares	868	0.88
Employees	4.404	4.47
Management	387	0.4
Domestic investors	5.166	5.25
Total	98.400	100.0

Source: SPH.

MOL employees are unlikely to be compensated for lost dividends by higher bonuses resulting from higher company profits. The domestic investors are mainly private investors, banks, and investment companies. All three investor groups are motivated by higher capital gains, so they are not expected to be deterred by lower dividends. With this background, the third phase of MOL privatization was completed in 1997, when the SPH sold an other large block of shares through the BSE.

In 1996, the effects of the first two privatization phases could already be felt in the operation of MOL. Simultaneously with privatization, new management was appointed. All this had a positive effect on company decisions, resulting in a series of innovative steps. The company set a strategic objective of making its presence felt in the markets of neighboring countries. To this end, MOL embarked on a filling station construction campaign, to be advanced progressively in the 1997–2000 period. Another innovative idea of the new management was to start exploration abroad—jointly with a U.S. multinational oil company—in the concession form. The internal information and IT systems were totally refurbished, accompanied by the building of a state-of-the-art integrated information system. Another strategic objective was to ensure the safe level of Hungarian oil and gas distribution. To this end, new agreements were concluded to link up the country with the oil and gas pipelines of Western Europe.

Privatization contributed to making MOL—apart from being the largest—one of the most efficient Hungarian companies.

2.2. Privatization of MATÁV

MATÁV was the first Hungarian company of strategic significance to get into majority foreign ownership. In asset size, MATÁV is the third-largest company in Hungary, while it ranks fourth in sales. Prior to 1993, the least developed countries in European telecommunications were Albania, Romania, and Hungary.

In the first phase of privatization (end of 1993), the state sold 30.14 percent of its shares in MATÁV. MagyarCom, a German–U.S. consortium, won the tender. The two members of the consortium are Deutsche Telekom and Ameritech International, both global telecommunications companies. In addition to MagyarCom, IFC acquired 0.99 percent and EBRD 1.97 percent in the company. In the first phase of privatization, Hungarian small-scale investors bought 2.04 percent of the shares. These investors are partly MATÁV employees and partly the municipalities whose territory is used by MATÁV for its operations.

In the 1993–95 period, MATÁV spent almost $1.2 billion for the development of the telephone network. According to the concession contract, the company has to invest another $700 million in the 1996–97 period, mostly in areas where the majority of households have no telephone and where no other solution was at hand. These areas are the most recession-stricken, and consequently a very slow return is expected on telecommunication investments. The privatization process enabled MATÁV to conclude concession contracts with global foreign companies possessing great amounts of capital. Thanks to these agreements, telecommunication improved dramatically in Hungary.

Table 16 shows the ownership structure of the company after the first phase of privatization, completed at the end of 1993.

In December 1995, the SPH completed the second phase of the privatization of MATÁV. In this second phase, MagyarCom purchased 2,050,565 strategic shares and 1,800,000 IPO shares. The SPH sold the two blocks of shares to MagyarCom for more than $852 million in cash. This brought the holdings of MagyarCom in MATÁV to 67.35 percent while those of the SPH were reduced to 28.14 percent + 1 share.

In the first phase of privatization (end of 1993), MATÁV was a vir-

60

Table 16

Ownership Structure of MATÁV, End of 1993

Shareholder	Type of share	No.	HUF '000	Business share
SPH	B	1	10	0.00%
SPH	A	6,727,363	67,273,630	64.86%
MagyarCom	A	3,126,845	31,268,450	30.14%
IFC	A	102,220	1,022,200	0.99%
EBRD	A	204,441	2,044,410	1.97%
Other		211,947	2,119,470	2.04%
Total		10,372,817	103,728,170	100.00%

Source: SPH.

tual monopoly in the Hungarian telecommunication sector. In the beginning of 1994, the monopoly was eliminated by the sale of local telecommunication concessions in eighteen regions of the country. The eighteen regions together represent 20 percent of the telecommunication market of the country. However, MATÁV did not lose 20 percent of the Hungarian telecommunication market, because a part of the revenue generated by the domestic and international sales in the eighteen regions remained with the company in the form of fees paid for services rendered. Altogether, MATÁV only lost 15 percent of its domestic telecommunication market to the regional companies.

In 1996 the third phase of the privatization of MATÁV was completed when employees bought up 278,833 shares. The transaction resulted in almost full compliance with the Privatization Act, which stipulated that only 25 percent of shares + 1 share could be kept permanently in state hands. To fully comply with the provisions of the law, the SPH would sell another block of shares (0.45 percent) in 1997.

With this sale, the privatization of MATÁV was practically completed and MagyarCom became the majority owner. MagyarCom consists of strategic investors who are not expected to part with their shares in the long run. The financial investors (EBRD, IFC) only have small blocks of shares, which are expected to be sold within five years.

The three-phase privatization of MATÁV brought in more than $17.7 billion to the Treasury, making it the largest Hungarian privatization. In the area of telecommunication, privatization brought fast and significant improvement into the farthest corners of the country. Privatization also enabled the company to conclude local concession contracts, which forced MATÁV to compete, at least in the domestic market. The amazing growth of the mobile phone market also contributed to the growth of competition. The most important results of the privatization of MATÁV were the significant growth of investments, great improvements in the efficiency of company management, and the streamlining of the company's structure.

2.3. Privatization of the Power Industry

The power industry in Hungary consists of eight power plants, six power distribution companies, the National Electric Works Company (MVM), and the National Power Grid Company. The functioning of the Hungarian power industry can be expressed in the following manner: power generated by the eight power plants is sold by the wholesaler (MVM) to the power distribution companies, which in turn sell power to households and businesses.

At the end of 1995, the government decided to privatize the Hungarian power sector. The SPH decided to arrange the privatization through a closed tendering process. Basically, Western European strategic investors were invited to bid and the winners were mostly German, Italian, and French state-owned power companies. In the course of privatization nine companies were sold; two power plants, six power distribution companies, and a design company. The last was sold off completely, while roughly 50 percent of the eight production and distribution companies were sold. Table 17 shows the state shares sold, the purchase price, and the foreign investors.

Table 18 shows the ownership structure of the Hungarian power sector after phase one of privatization.

At the end of 1995, the sale of the power industry generated privatization revenue of roughly $1.3 billion for the Treasury. Privatization revenue was mostly in foreign currency. Employee ownership acquisition was limited to ETV-Eröterv Design Company, where E-loans and compensation certificates were used. The strategic investors were German (Bavarian), French, and Italian power companies owned by the state or by a province. The privatization contracts contained options for the investors to purchase further blocks of shares from the SPH in the future, at December 1995

Table 17

Privatization of the Power Industry

Company	Equity (HUF)	Company share sold (%)	Purchase price (%)	Investor
Budapest Power Distribution Co.	61,739,916	46.15	178	RWE-EVS consortium
Southern Transdanubia Power Distribution Co.	30,566,241	47.25	107	Bayernwerk AG
Southern Hungary Power Distribution Co.	38,739,089	47.98	122	Electricité de France
Danube Power Plant Co.	36,069,743	48.76	120	Powerfin -Tractebel consortium
Northern Transdanubia Power Distribution Co.	51,460,861	47.55	123	Electricité de France
Northern Hungary Power Distribution Co.	30,957,648	48.81	154	RWE-EVS consortium
Matra Power Plant Co.	36,441,910	38.09	79	RWE-EVS consortium
Transtisza Power Distribution Co.	34,347,755	49.23	109	Isar-Amperewerke AG
ETV-Eröterv Design Co.	769,968	89.60	105	IVO International

Source: SPH.

share prices. Consequently it is expected that in the 1997–2000 period these strategic investors will acquire majorities everywhere in the Hungarian power sector. It could also happen, of course, that the strategic investors would sell off their block of shares (or a part of it) to another strategic or portfolio investor.

At present, it is too early to evaluate the results of the privatization of the Hungarian power industry. Most independent experts think, however, that this privatization will have negative effects, thanks to the monopoly position of the power companies sold in the domestic market. Globally, it is almost unheard of that a state should sell off its majority share in a power sector having a monopoly position in the domestic market. The only other reported case is Argentina. However, the foreign strategic investors pledged new investments in the power industry worth almost $3 billion. These investments are expected to occur in the 1997–2002 period, which should have positive effects on economic growth.

Table 18

Ownership of the Hungarian Power Sector after the First Phase of Privatization

	Registered capital of company	Share of SPH	Share of National Electricity Corporation	Share of other owners
Power distribution companies				
Budapest Power Distribution Co.	60,744,410	30,372,205	10	30,372,195
South Transdanubian Power Distribution Co.	29,797,710	14,898,855	10	14,898,845
South Hungarian Power Distribution Co.	37,029,110	18,514,555	10	18,514,545
North Transdanubian Power Distribution Co.	46,441,155	23,441,155	10	23,441,145
North Hungarian Power Distribution Co.	30,504,210	15,252,105	10	15,252,095
Transtisza Power Distribution Co.	34,158,510	17,079,255	10	17,079,245
Total	239,116,260	119,558,130	60	119,558,070
Power plants				
Bakony Power Plant Co.	16,227,240	5,516,590	5,629,100	5,081,550
Budapest Power Plant Co.	14,366,510	5,982,740	7,183,250	1,200,520
Danube Power Plant Co.	33,542,230	10	16,771,110	16,771,110
Matra Power Plant Co.	34,245,640	10	13,095,700	21,149,930
Paks Nuclear Power Plant Co.	126,598,810	10	126,399,680	199,120
Pécs Power Plant Co.	14,807,800	6,008,720	6,488,700	2,310,460
Tisza Power Plant Co.	34,745,610	17,271,160	17,372,800	101,650
Vértes Power Plant Co.	22,787,440	8,820,680	9,001,700	4,965,060
Total	297,321,360	43,599,920	201,942,040	51,779,400
Others				
National Power Grid Co.	4,522,610	0	4,193,680	328,930
ETV-Erőterv Design Co.	646,180	0	0	646,180
MVM Co.	249,608,400	249,161,990	0	446,410
Total	786,046,020	412,320,040	201,942,100	171,783,880

Source: SPH.

2.4. Privatization of Regional Gas Distribution Companies

In Hungary there are five regional gas distribution companies. The government decided that the privatization process should be organized at the end of 1995 in the form of a multiple round public bid. In each gas distribution company, the majority share would be sold, representing 50 percent shares + 1 share.

According to the privatization concept elaborated by the government, the new owners should be strategic investors, sizable in their own country (distributing gas to at least 100,000 households), that can meet several requirements relating to financial reliability. Table 19 shows the results of privatization of the five regional gas distribution companies.

Table 19

Privatization of Regional Gas Companies

Company name	Investor name	Price %
DDGÁZ Co.	Ruhrgas AGVEW AG. consortium	270.8%
DÉGÁZ Co.	Gaz de France	206.2%
ÉGÁZ Co.	Gaz de France	431.1%
TIGÁZ Co.	Italgas S.p.A-S.N.A.M. S.p.A consortium	282.1%
KÖGÁZ Co.	Bayernwerk AG-EVN Energie AG. Consortium	282.3%

Source: SPH.

The table shows that all the winners were Western European state-owned gas distribution companies. It is, as yet, difficult to evaluate the success of this privatization. However a great many doubts have been expressed by Hungarian experts, who question the advisability of selling off whole sectors—which are virtual monopolies in the domestic market—to foreign state companies. The state could have achieved its long-term results (investments, efficiency growth, link-up with the Western European power networks) without privatization, avoiding losses and problems that are expected to be created by the future exploitation of the monopoly position.

3. Completion of Privatization

According to the Privatization Act, privatization had to be completed by the end of 1997. A part of the transactions were expected to be completed only in the first half of 1998, when the privatization process was expected to be completed. Thus Hungarian privatization, which started in 1987, will have taken twelve years to complete.

Privatization will continue with municipality-owned enterprises, and after 1998 the municipalities can be regarded as the main players in the decentralized privatization process. The market value of assets owned by almost 3,200 municipalities (utility companies, land, blocks of shares, etc.) is very difficult to estimate. In addition, these assets are expected to increase in value continuously after 1998, when the Hungarian economy should have passed the transformation crisis and have attained, at first modest and later, dynamic economic growth.

Sustained economic growth will raise the general value of assets owned by municipalities and the value of blocks of shares and land in particular. The value of assets of municipality-owned utility could increase once the income status of inhabitants living in the given region improves. However, the future value of municipality-owned assets is expected to show a significant variation in the different regions of Hungary. In the case of towns located in northern Transdanubia and in and around the capital (Gödöllö, Esztergom, Kecskemét, and Eger), the market value of locally owned assets could grow significantly. In the northeastern and Transitisza regions of Hungary and on the Great Plain the value of local assets could even decrease. For foreign and domestic investors both the increase and decrease of the value of local assets represent good investment opportunities. For example, Hungarian land is valued presently at a mere 4 percent of the price of Bavarian land.

In the final phase of privatization, the new power sector owners (German, French, and Italian state-owned power companies) have an option to purchase the majority blocks of shares. It is highly probable that they will exercise this option and purchase a majority share in the Hungarian energy sector in 1998. As only Western European companies won the bids, the sale of shares to U.S. and Asian investors, in certain cases, cannot be ruled out.

The SPH must hand over 40 percent of the shares of the gas distribution companies and 25 percent of the shares of the power distribution companies to the municipalities. After 1998, the municipalities may sell these blocks of shares partly to strategic, partly to portfolio, investors. Mainly foreign investors may purchase blocks of shares from the municipalities. Even now, there are signs that Hungarian and foreign brokerages are negotiating with the municipalities on the sale of shares—to be sold later to foreign investors.

The privatization of the water distribution sector is predominantly under the control of the municipalities. The French CGE already has a 47 percent share int he Pécs Water Works, and Western European companies show great interest in the privatization of Budapest Water Works and other local water distribution companies. In the forthcoming year the Budapest municipality could collect privatization revenue of 150 to 250 million dollars for the sale of water distribution rights. The revenue of local municipalities is expected to be much lower.

In the chemical industry, the SPH will sell off its 30 percent share in MOL in the final phase of privatization, and the sale of Taurus is expected in 1997. Minor blocks of shares of Richter Pharmaceuticals and Borsodchem will also be sold. As for these latter companies, the new owners are expected to be foreign strategic and portfolio investors. In the 1997–98 period, Nitrokémia and Tisza Chemical Works would also be privatized, to be sold most probably to foreign strategic investors, but foreign portfolio investors also have a chance during privatization. In the 1977–98 period, foreign investments amounting to almost $400 million were expected during the privatization of the chemical industry.

In the machine industry, there are two important companies left in state hands, Ikarus and Rába. The privatization concept of the two companies has not been decided yet. Two opinions prevail: maintaining independence and leaving control in domestic hands, and selling off to foreign strategic investors.

In the food industry, only a few companies are left in state hands. These are expected to be privatized in exchange for compensation certificates. Later on, after restructuring, the Hungarian investors are expected to sell off the companies to foreign strategic investors.

In the financial sector, the privatization of the Commercial Bank is expected in 1997–98. Several medium-sized banks would probably be sold in the 1997–98 period, mostly to large Hungarian-owned banks (OTP, MFB Company, Postabank). In the 1997–2000 period, new financial institutions will be established for mortgage credits in the areas of business, agriculture, and housing. When establishing new financial institutions, the government relies upon foreign investors.

In the final phase of privatization, the SPH will sell off its holdings in companies where the state still has a minority stake (e.g. Borsod Brewery, Pannonia Hotels, Cable Works). In these cases, foreign investors could play the main roles. The SPH has a minority share in several food industrial companies (e.g., in the sugar industry), which could be purchased by Hungrian manufacturers in exchange for compensation certificates.

4. Privatization and the "Disappearance" of State Assets

In 1990—the year in which politically and administratively supported and centrally controlled privatization began—all political, government, and business protagonists participating in the process thought that the main procedure of eliminating state ownership would be privatization. Today, at the end of 1997, we can assert that they were wrong. In 1990 the asset value of state-owned companies, according to their balance sheet, was approximately 2,000 billion forints, to which a further 1,000 billion forints should be added as the value of land ignored by the balance sheets. The adjusted value of state-owned assets is 12,000 billion forints today. Figures 4 and 5 show the change of state-owned assets.

Now we confront the oddest phenomenon of the economy after the change of regime. The state was unable to control the privatization of the bulk of its assets, which occurred mostly through other channels. *Privatization* is not the right expression for this process; rather, one should call it the accumulation of private capital. Nonetheless, the political and economic studies analyzing the creation of the private sector deal almost exclusively with privatization, usually neglecting those processes outside of privatization that actually contributed to the creation of the private sector.

In addition to centrally controlled privatization, there were three major economic processes turning state assets private. Of these, the capital loss of state-owned enterprises seems by far the most important. Capital loss occurs when market value—being typically dissimilar to the value according to the balance sheet—shrinks from one year to the next. No data are available that show the accurate extent of capital loss of state-owned enterprises. But if the extent is unknown, the main reasons are mostly clear. The first main reason was the loss of foreign and domestic markets. State-owned enterprises suffered losses not only in foreign markets but also in the domestic market. This was partly due to the fact that liberaliza-

Figure 4

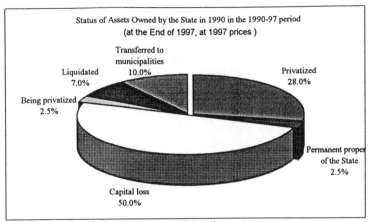

Status of Assets Owned by the State in 1990 in the 1990-97 period
(at the End of 1997, at 1997 prices)

Transferred to
municipalities
10.0%

Liquidated
7.0%

Privatized
28.0%

Being privatized
2.5%

Permanent proper
of the State
2.5%

Capital loss
50.0%

Source: Privatization Research Institute.

Figure 5

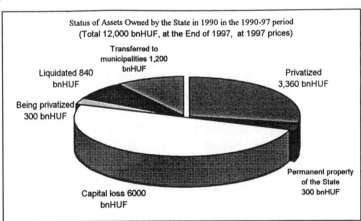

Status of Assets Owned by the State in 1990 in the 1990-97 period
(Total 12,000 bnHUF, at the End of 1997, at 1997 prices)

Transferred to
municipalities 1,200
bnHUF

Liquidated 840
bnHUF

Privatized
3,360 bnHUF

Being privatized
300 bnHUF

Permanent property
of the State
300 bnHUF

Capital loss 6000
bnHUF

Source: Privatization Research Institute.

tion of imports created a real market environment in the economy, confronting pampered state-owned enterprises with strong competition. The loss of monopoly positions in internal markets caused profitability to decrease, thus shrinking asset value. In addition to market loss, state-owned enterprises continuously lost their best professionals and managers, attracted by a much more generously paying private sector. As to assets missing from the balance sheet—intellectual capital, research and development capacity, corporate image, market position, etc.—the changes were even more significant than those of the assets disclosed in the balance sheet. As a result, the beginning of the 1990s became the turning point; while earlier the market value of state-owned enterprises was bigger than their book value, after that date the ratio was inverted. The market value of enterprises started to shrink below their book value.

It cannot be suggested that asset values would have held up if the amounts for fixed asset replacements substituted for the missing amortization. Accepting the lower efficiency of a state-owned enterprise due to the lack of owner interest, it is only fair to admit that even if a correct amortization system had been in place, the real asset value of state-owned enterprises would still have suffered losses in the 1990–95 period. However, one can be fairly sure that, from a privatization aspect, the state-owned enterprises would have been in a much better position, then and in 1997, had they accounted properly for amortization costs, using the amounts to meet real fixed assets replacement needs. National company income generated wages and taxes, finally resulting in consumption. Since state-owned enterprises also suffered losses in the home market, it can be stated that consumer purchasing power, in the form of wages and (through the redistribution of the state budget) additional household income, generated by non–accounted for amortization, basically created demand for the private sector. Consequently, the non–accounted for amortizaton of state-owned enterprises served finally in the accumulation of private capital in the 1988–98 period.

5. The Fast Expansion of the Private Sector

Another consequence of the process was the weakening of the tax-paying and job-creating ability of state-owned enterprises and the simultaneous strengthening of the private sector, in both domestic firms and joint ventures. In Hungary, the particular nature of the transition to a market economy resulted in a private sector created in a masked, secretive way. In the 1957–90 period, private activity could only function in latent opposition to politics and administration. Consequently, tax evasion became a national obsession. As soon as private small-scale enterprises started to function as real companies, their tax obligations spiraled upward and—at least prior to 1990—their operational safety even deteriorated. After 1990, the picture remained the same, because the political change of regime caused no breakthrough in the tax system.

The tax burden remained unacceptably high for the private companies, creating a very tough environment compared to the earlier situation, but also in comparison with the West. No wonder that the dynamically growing private sector refused to lose its secretive nature, at least as far as taxation was concerned. This was the source of the oddity of the Hungarian economic transition. In terms of economic performance, the unbelievably fast demise of the state sector was almost counterbalanced by the extremely fast growth of the private sector. From the state-budget point of view, a lack of equilibrium prevailed. The reduction of the tax-paying and job-creating abilities of the state sector caused the Treasury to lose revenue without receiving compensation in the form of more taxes from the dynamically growing private sector. In fact, tax evasion was one of the drivers of this dynamism.

In the 1990s, the capital loss of state-owned enterprises functioned as the source of private capital accumulation. There was another important form of creating a private sector; the establishment of new companies, evading both privatization and the influx of foreign capital. Of the $16 billion of FDI, roughly $5 billion can be linked to the privatization processes. The rest financed the establishment of new companies. We do not have figures for the exact proportions of the participation of domestic private capital in privatization and in the establishment of new companies. Experience and calculations show, however, that only a small fraction participated in the privatizaton processes and significantly more turned toward the establishment of new companies or the capital expansion of already-existing private companies.

However, there was another reason for the establishment and expansion of private companies rather than privatization to be the typical process of the transition to market economy. Due to the seeds of capitalism and capital accumulation sown prior to the 1990 change of regime, entrepreneurs already had ready-made strategies and techniques at their disposal to establish and run private companies.

A premise of organization theory is that it is always easier to establish a new organization than to restructure an existing one. Perhaps this is why both foreign and domestic entrepreneurs stopped making efforts to purchase state assets even when these assets were offered at more realistic prices. Instead, they followed strategies and techniques allowing them to build a successful company cheaper and faster. They chose to remain potential buyers of state assets offered for privatization. This meant that foreign and domestic investors preferred privatization to green field investment only if a segment of the domestic market could not be acquired other than through privatization.

Both processes—capital loss and the establishment or expansion of private companies bypassing privatization—were faster and of greater volume than privatization itself. The reason for this was that both had stronger roots and more familiar strategies and techniques than privatization. The process of capital loss of state-owned enterprises did not start in 1990 but much earlier, in the 1980s. As early as 1982, the newly established private companies started to suck the lifeblood out of the state-owned enterprises, including intellectual capital, the best professionals, markets, and products. The distortions of the accounting and tax system in the 1980s caused state-owned enterprises to accumulate significant replacement shortages. In the beginning of the 1990s, these two processes gained strength and the change of regime gave political and economic momentum to the development of foreign and domestic private capital. This was the period when double-digit inflation turned capital loss into a veritable snowball rolling down a slope.

The Peculiar Road of the Transition to a Market Economy in Hungary

It seems reasonable to state that after the 1990 change of regime, centrally controlled privatization was overtaken by several other processes that affected more actors and had a greater influence on the transition to market economy than the privatization process.

While the establishment and expansion of private companies by foreign and domestic investors must be regarded, on balance, as positive developments, noncontrolled privatization and capital loss require a subtler evaluation. In Hungary, the transition to a market economy took place in the context of the country's historical roots and the distortions in the privatization environment. This placed the establishment and expansion of private companies, rather than privatization, at the center of the creation of the private sector. The process was implemented, however, in a most contradictory manner, because while the state sector stopped assuming the task of balancing the state budget, the new private sector refused to do so. The state sector was dismantled during the process of capital loss—which could be regarded mostly as spontaneous. Therefore, although a private sector came into existence, which was of the same magnitude as the state sector in asset value, economic performance, and employment, it was still secretive in the old way and, most important, refused to assume the social burdens of transition. This process became exacerbated in 1994, when the state budget deficit reached 7 to 8 percent of official GDP and the deficit of the balance of payments was almost $4 billion. In fact, economic performance was much better in 1994, as the real GDP growth rate (5–5.5 percent) was much higher than the officially published figure of 2.5 percent. By the same token, the official deficit of the balance of payments could have been 2.5 to 3 billion dollars less without capital flight.

While the pace of privatization was relatively slow, the private sector was growing and expanding really quickly. Had privatization alone been used to eliminate state ownership and foster the accumulation of private capital, the creation of the private sector could never have been so dynamic. The scarcity of available capital resources would have stood in the way. The three processes together—capital loss of state-owned enterprises, privatization, and the very fast creation of the private sector—resulted in an economy in which macroeconomic equilibrium disappears, but adaptation is thorough and fast on a microeconomic level. Within the given accounting and tax environment, the capital loss of state-owned enterprises could be limited exclusively by privatization.

The volume of privatization, however, was much smaller than the volume of capital loss, and privatization was unable to compensate the Treasury for lost tax revenue through new taxes paid by the new owners of privatization assets. Thus in the middle of the 1990s the peculiar Hungarian form of the transition to market economy sank into equilibrium crisis.

It can be regarded as symbolic that the political tension—linked to macroeconomical disequilibrium—during the transition process was caused by privatization. Large-volume capital loss linked to slow privati-

73

zation had a very negative effect on company profits through heavy taxation. Profits and tax revenues shrank, causing the huge deficit of the state budget. The private sector defended its interests against the state by capital flight. The process grew gradually until the end of 1994, when capital flight reached alarming proportions, thus causing huge deficits in the trade balance and in the balance of payments. Capital flight took diverse forms. Overbilling imports, underbilling exports, and settlement prices used between the foreign and domestic units of international companies were utilized to transfer most of the profits abroad, bypassing statistics and evading taxation. The process was also stimulated by an overvalued currency. In a fully liberalized foreign trade environment, the only way to curb imports was through a strong local currency, while exports were not stimulated at all, neither through the exchange rate nor through other monetary and economic policies. In addition in 1994, a new coalition government took office, which showed hesitation in the area of privatization. Consequently, by the beginning of 1995 the achievements of the transition period became devalued in the eyes of the international business community, the national image abruptly deteriorated, and in the spring of 1995 the government was forced to introduce restrictive measures to curb consumption. The period of transition in Hungary had one peculiar feature, which was that privatization was unable to gather momentum due to its politicization, which finally resulted in the risk of a political crisis.

7. Political, Macro-, and Microeconomic Evaluation

To evaluate the success of the past four years of privatization it is advisable to desegregate the political, macro-, and microeconomic aspects. From a political aspect, privatization can doubtless be regarded as a success. Part of this success was due to the fact that after the change of regime all-important political forces agreed—and agree today—with denationalization, the near-elimination of state ownership, and the strengthening of private ownership. The process was also a political success because, in spite of the serious controversy between the parties of the first coalition government, for four years a stable political environment was ensured to serve as a safe basis for the transition to a market economy. The process was a political success also because—except for the serious slowing down of the election year (1994)—privatization was never stopped. It continued, in spite of its clumsiness and technical limits, for four years within a professional channel. As a consequence, in the 1990–94 period even if privatization served to sour cooperation among the ruling political elite, in spite of the different skirmishes of a political nature, privatization basically remained a professional issue.

From a macroeconomic point of view, privatization seems a very negative process. It was too slow to hinder or slow down the capital loss process of state-owned enterprises. It was unable to offer the additional revenue to the Treasury required to finance the development of the new physical and human infrastructure necessitated by the new market economy environment. The slowness and limited scope of privatization meant that state-owned enterprises were unable to gain access to additional capital sources, thus making privatization, in addition to the accounting and tax system, one of the reasons that state asset loss became so overwhelming. At the same time, privatization cannot be blamed alone—or even primarily—for the disappearance of macroeconomic equilibrium. The real culprit is economic policy, which failed to recognize the real processes of the transition period. No attempt was made to stop the disappearance of state assets—through the accounting and tax system, the investment policy, the exchange rate policy, and other measures—until a private sector was created that had a tax-paying and job-creating ability at least similar to that of the gradually becoming defunct state sector.

For all practical purposes, economic policy abandoned the actors of the transition to market economy, simultaneously failing to protect state-owned enterprises and render assistance to the private sector. The actors were left alone to find their way in a wild capitalist free-market environment. Although all actors were abandoned in a similar manner, economic policy was still discriminating, because it left no escape path for state-owned enterprises (e.g., through fast privatization with simultaneous equity increase), while private companies could retain profits through tax evasion. Today it is clear that economic policy should have better protected the state sector. It should have reinforced job creation and profit-generating ability through fast privatization with simultaneous equity increase, industry protection, export stimulation, and significant tax cuts, while the new private sector should have been forced to assume its public burden. Of course, all this would have only been possible after a radical tax cut. Such a step could have offered better protection for the state sector competing with the foreign and domestic private sector, simultaneously giving an impetus to foreign and domestic private entrepreneurs to legalize profits.

On a microeconomic level, privatization must be considered more as a success than a failure. The reason for this is that the adaptation and competitiveness of the economy proved to be significantly better than reflected by macroeconomic indicators, this in spite of decreasing industrial production, fast-growing luxury consumption, an alarmingly shrinking manufacturing sector, and a too-quickly-expanding service sector. By 1995 a strong market economy was in place. The actual proportion of the private sector reached 65 to 70 percent, the proportion of tax-evading sectors—according to estimates—was as high as 30 percent of GDP. GDP, corrected for hidden incomes and foreign capital flight, reached $60 billion at the same time. The profitability of the GDP grew significantly (which served, in turn, as the source of a capital flight that was estimated in 1994 to be as high as $3 billion). All other qualitative indicators of the economy show significant improvement on a microeconomic level.

Although in the long run the pluses and minuses of the political, macro-, and microeconomic aspects of privatization and the transition to market economy balance each other, in the short and medium run they lead to cyclical crisis. In my opinion, a deliberate economic policy could have put transition on a slightly modified orbit at the time of changing the regime. This policy could have focused on fast privatization with simultaneous equity increase, large investments in physical and human infrastructure, and multifaceted and deliberate export stimulation. The slow buildup of the private sector, however, startling almost as early as 1957, drove economic policy. The transition process left the market actors almost abandoned to act in a spontaneous manner, and the private sector was allowed to grow in a secretive and masked way. The state sector—which had assumed a dominant role in the past in the creation of jobs and payments to the state budget—was first protected less and then finally not at all. This was the dilemma of the autumn of 1990, when the issues of internal and foreign policy finally gained the upper hand over economic policy and economic issues. Thus the radical renewal of economic policy was taken off the agenda.

The various periods of privatization can be categorized as follows: The period of preparation lasted for decades, from 1957 to the beginning of the 1980s. The creation of the private sector took almost a decade, in the 1980s, and spontaneous privatization was a direct preparation phase lasting for four or five years. The first phase of privatization took four years and was accompanied by the disappearance of almost 50 percent of state assets in the form of capital loss. After the second phase, privatization would be completed in 1998, with capital loss showing a decreasing tendency.

5

The Role of Foreign Capital in Privatization

A special feature of Hungarian privatization was the significant role played by foreign capital. By the end of 1996, almost half of all foreign investment (direct investments and owners' loans together, amounting to a total of $5.25 billion) targeted privatization and the other half chose greenfield investments. Almost 40 percent of all FDI that targeted the region (the Czech Republic, Slovakia, Poland, Hungary, Romania, and Slovenia) ended up in Hungary.

Until the end of 1995, the country maintained that advantage, and in two years (1992 and 1993) that proportion even reached 60 percent. By the end of 2000, Poland and the Czech Republic are expected to have caught up with Hungary. Hungary expects to receive between $1.5 to $2 billion each year until the end of the century.

1. Distribution of FDI

The distribution of FDI according to country of origin shows a strong concentration. The first four countries (Germany, the USA, Austria, and France) represent more than 70 percent of all investments. Until the end of 1994, the United States was on top of the list, due to the fact that at the beginning of the 1990s General Electric, General Motors, Ford, and Guardian Glass invested significant sums in Hungary. In 1995 Germany took over the first rank and France caught up with Austria. Both were due to the privatization of the energy sector, in which German and French companies played a decisive role. The high ranking of Austria was due to its geographic advantage and the traditional Austro-Hungarian links. To date—at least in terms of its role played in the global economy and especially in international investments—Japan has shown surprisingly little interest in Hungary.

From 1994 the proportion of portfolio investments grew. This was due to the increased activity of EBRD and certain investment funds, and the initial public offering of several large Hungarian companies (like MOL, Richter, and the OTP Bank). Figure 6 and Table 20 show the distribution of FDI according to country of origin and the trends in the first half of the 1990s.

At the beginning of the 1990s, FDI concentrated on manufacturing. Later on, when telecommunication and power production and distribution became privatized and concessions were sold, the proportion of manufacturing to the total shrank. It was evident from the end of 1993 that foreign investments targeted the purchase of the Hungarian monopolies. Foreign investments made a significant contribution to the modernization of industry, partly in the area of electronics and telecommunication, partly by the creation of a modern new sector—car manufacturing. Figure 7 and table 21 shows the sectoral distribution of FDI in the first half of the 1990s.

The significance of foreign investments can be well illustrated by the fact that out of the top 200 Hungarian companies almost 110 are under the control of full or partial foreign owners. At the end of 1995, the number of companies with majority foreign ownership was 98 within the top 200, and by the end of 1996 this figure rose to 120. As table 22 shows, at the end of 1996 the number of companies with some form of foreign ownership was 134 within the top 200. According to certain forecasts, the number of companies with some form of foreign ownership will grow within the top 200 by the end of the 2000 period, mainly due to the fact that some domestic private owners will sell off their shares to foreign investors.

Privatization has another peculiar feature. Twenty-five percent ($3.3 billion) of all foreign investments belong to state or parastate investors. Major state-owned foreign investors are Deutsche Telekom; German, French, and Italian power companies; Italian and Austrian banks and metallurgical companies; and power stations owned by German states.

FDI is strongly concentrated in the northwestern part of Hungary, the capital and the region around the capital. At the end of 1996, 46 percent of foreign investments had come to the capital and the surrounding region (Pest County) and 26 percent to four counties in northern Transdanubia. More than 70 percent of foreign investments targeted the capital and regions constituting less than 30 percent of the country, while the balance was distributed in areas making up more than 70 percent of the country. This phenomenon is shown in figure 9. Greenfield investments show an even greater concentration: 85 percent of such investments targeted Pest

Figure 6

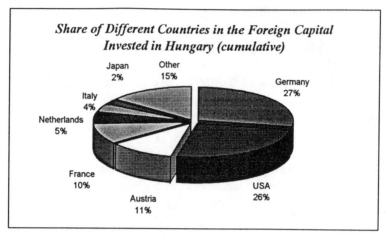

Share of Different Countries in the Foreign Capital Invested in Hungary (cumulative)

Japan 2%
Other 15%
Italy 4%
Netherlands 5%
France 10%
Austria 11%
Germany 27%
USA 26%

Source: Privatization Research Institute.

Table 20

Share of Certain Countries in the Foreign Investments in Hungary
(Cumulative, in %)

Until May 1993	(%)	Until December 1994	(%)	Until December 1995	(%)	Until December 1996	(%)
1. USA	29.0	1. USA	27.0	1. Germany	29.0	1. Germany	28.0
2. Germany	19.5	2. Germany	24.5	2. USA	24.0	2. USA	26.0
3. Austria	13.5	3. Austria	13.4	3. Austria	10.5	3. Austria	10.5
4. France	7.0	4. France	6.8	4. France	9.0	4. France	10.0
5. Italy	6.0	5. Italy	5.0	5. Italy	4.0	5. Netherlands	4.5
6. Japan	4.5	6. Britain	5.0	6. Netherlands	4.0	6. Italy	4.0
						Japan	2.2
Without portfolio investment		Without portfolio investment		Portfolio investments 8		Portfolio investments 8.5	
				Together with EBRD and IFC		Together with EBRD and IFC	

Source: Privatization Research Institute.

Figure 7

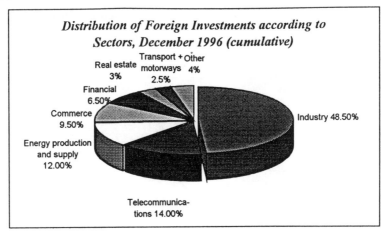

Distribution of Foreign Investments according to Sectors, December 1996 (cumulative)

- Transport + Other motorways 4%
- Real estate 3%
- 2.5%
- Financial 6.50%
- Commerce 9.50%
- Energy production and supply 12.00%
- Telecommunications 14.00%
- Industry 48.50%

Source: Privatization Research Institute.

Table 21

Distribution of Foreign Investments among Individual Sectors
(cumulative, in %)

	May 1993			*December 1994*			*December 1995*			*December 1996*	
1.	Industry	66	1.	Industry	57	1.	Industry	50	1.	Industry	48.5
2.	Finance	10	2.	Telecom	14	2.	Telecom	15	2.	Telecom	14.0
3.	Commerce	9	3.	Finance	8	3.	Power		3.	Power	
4.	Real estate,		4.	Commerce	7		production			production	
	office and other		5.	Real estate	7		and supply	13		and supply	12.0
	buildings	7				4.	Finance	6	4.	Commerce	9.5
5.	Telecom	1				5.	Commerce	6	5.	Finance	6.5
	Other	7					Other	10	6.	Real estate	3.0
									7.	Transport and motorways	6.5

Source: Privatization Research Institute.

Table 22

Foreign Owned Companies among the Hungarian Top 200

	December 1995	*December 1996*
Number of companies with majority foreign ownership	98	120
Number of companies with minority foreign ownership	8	7
Number of companies owned by foreign financial and other institutions (portfolio)	5	7
Total	111	134

Source: Figyelő Top 200.

Figure 8

Source: Figyelő Top 200.

County and northern Transdanubia. The review of geographical distribution of foreign investments shows that foreign investors prefer towns along or near the Vienna–Budapest line if linked by a motorway or first-class road and towns with significant industrial traditions. Foreign investors avoided regions not linked by motorways, towns within the rust belt (northeastern Hungary), and regions far off the Vienna–Budapest line. The structure of foreign investments also shows that Budapest and its surroundings are very attractive to investors. This supports the concept of Budapest becoming a true regional investment and commercial center in Central Europe, after Vienna.

2. Motivations of Foreign Investors

Foreign investors can be grouped into three types. The first type is motivated by the acquisition of market. Here the investment objective is to grab the highest possible share in the domestic market by taking over companies or by establishing new ones. Investments of this first type can be found in commerce, the financial sector, telecommunications, energy, the real estate sector, and manufacturing of consumer goods targeting the Hungarian market only. Sixty to sixty-five percent of investments belong to the first type. The second type of investor is attracted by low production costs. A trend prevails in the West, where due to the high local wages and incidental costs manufacturing moves to countries where wages and costs are lower. Another reason for the move can be pollution, which is strongly regulated in the West, thus making production increasingly expensive. The so-called portfolio investors represent the third type. These are investment and pension funds and other institutional investors that—expecting rising share prices and ample dividends—buy up shares of local public companies. For example, the privatized MOL, OTP Bank, Richter Pharmaceuticals, Borsodchem, and TVK were all portfolio investments. Portfolio investors tend not to interfere with company operations and management, being almost totally absorbed in the monitoring of market forecasts and profit data. They vote by the sale of their stocks or by the purchase of new ones. Within all foreign investments the role of portfolio investment is growing, while the number of new initial offerings unfortunately is dwindling. Certain emerging companies (e.g., Grabolast, Pannonplast, and Zalakerámia) acquire additional capital needs from the capital market by

Table 23

Distribution of Foreign Investments According to Regions
(cumulative, in %)

	Until May 1993	*Until Dec 1994*	*Until Dec 1995*	*Until Dec 1996*
1. Budapest (with Pest County)	51.0	49.0	46.0	46.0
2. Northern Transdanubia (Vas, Győr, Fejér, Komárom, and Veszprém Counties)	25.0	27.0	27.5	26.0
3. Great Plain (Bács, Csongrád, Békés, Szolnok, and Hajdú Counties)	13.0	12.0	13.0	12.0
4. Northeastern Hungary (Szabolcs, Borsod, Heves, and Nógrád Counties)	6.0	7.0	7.5	10.5
5. Southern Transdanubia (Zala, Somogy, Baranya, and Tolna Counties)	5.0	5.0	6.0	5.5

Source: Privatization Research Institute.

Figure 9

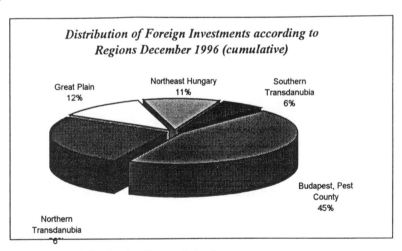

Source: Privatization Research Institute.

issuing new stocks. This so-called stock exchange privatization method allows Hungarian companies to preserve independence. Foreigners control 80 to 85 percent of stock turnover at the BSE.

3. Effects of Foreigners on Competition

Due to privatization, the corporate-ownership concentration increased in certain sectors. The role of oligopolies grew in road construction, the cement industry, PB and natural gas and power distribution, brick and tile manufacturing trade, sugar and paper industry, newspaper publication, printing, and several other sectors. In other sectors (e.g., banking and insurance, several food industrial sectors, and the machine industry), competition increased significantly. Trade was the sector in which the number of players grew, while a few foreign companies continuously increased their influence in the market. Due to the reduced size of the market and optimal levels of production, multicompetitor markets are very difficult to create in several industries. Here the only avenue open for true competition is through the liberalization of imports.

4. The Effect of Foreign Investments on Regional Development

Privatization-linked investments adjusted to the corporate-regional structure that had come into existence earlier. Privatization began in Budapest and Transdanubia, so local companies received capital injections earlier. The tendency of greenfield investments aiming at the conquest of the domestic market is to cover the whole country, but the first investments are always in Budapest and northern Transdanubia (retail trade, mobile phones). Of course, potential consumer demand affects concrete investment decisions. In the case of retail trade investments, the consumers of neighboring countries are also taken into account (e.g., Metro). The bulk of office-building investments is concentrated in Budapest. As to green field investments in manufacturing, two-thirds were established in northern Transdanubia. Another significant area is Pest County, and the position of Kecskemét has been growing recently. New jobs are being created primarily through greenfield investments, resulting in additional advantages for northern Transdanubia and Budapest and its surroundings. Foreign investments increase regional-economic differences even further. While in the first place, companies producing goods for Western exports set up in Transdanubia, Budapest, and its surroundings were preferred by investors targeting the Hungarian and the central Eastern European markets, establishing manufacturing and distribution bases. Whereas at the beginning of the 1990s the municipalities demanded significant funds from investors, today the situation is different. Municipalities offer preferentially priced land and other forms of stimulation just to attract foreign investors. The eastern counties are passive; e.g., ITT Automotive wished to set up in Nyíregyháza but was unable to buy the land. However, the municipalities of several towns (Gödöllö, Kechskemét) show fervent activity to court investors.

5. Foreign Investors in Agriculture

Agriculture is the least transparent and explored area. Due to the legal and political risks of land purchase, few privatization transactions were affected. The Szekszárd Agricultural Combine, a couple of state farms near Lake Balaton, and several vineyards in the Tokaj region were purchased by foreigners. It can be assumed that much more land became foreign property in the course of liquidation. According to my information, several Transdanubian co-ops also sold lands to foreigners. The private sale of lands is almost unknown at present. The new foreign owners completed significant development; e.g., almost $40 million was invested in the Tokaj region alone, with French, Spanish, and British investors present.

According to observers, significant speculative land purchases were effected in the course of the compensation process. At the same time, several foreign investors appeared in wine growing, the fruit and vegetable sector, gardening, and dairy farms. Many Hungarians living abroad purchased and started to cultivate land in Hungary. It is reported that the most significant foreign activity in agriculture can be seen in Györ, Zala, and Tolna Counties.

An important development has been the assistance rendered to undercapitalized suppliers of raw material (farmers) by foreign-owned food companies, through advances, grants, or other means. There are positive examples of this in the tobacco, sugar beet, and sunflower seed sectors.

6. Effect of Foreign Investments on Employment

The number of jobs with companies privatized by foreign professional investors was reduced by 5 to 20 percent. Even in companies where important new capacities were created (Tungsram, Lehel), the number of jobs declined. But this process has always been present, even after privatization by Hungarian investors.

Major foreign greenfield industrial investments (exceeding half a million dollars each) created almost 40,000 new jobs. It can be assumed that real estate lease, commerce, and the service sector created even more jobs than manufacturing. New industrial facilities typically employ between 20 and 200 people, with the exceptions of cable manufacturing, the apparel industry, and the manufacturing and assembly of electronic components.

Summary

Privatization in Hungary started in 1987 and was expected to be concluded in 1998. Since 1990 privatization has accelerated, and it reached its peak in 1995. Twenty percent of the property owned by the state in 1990 had been passed on to private ownership by 1996 through privatization. After 1998 long-term state ownership will be constituted 2 percent of state property as of 1990. This low figure precisely shows that in the next decade the majority of state property will be operated by owners belonging to the private sector. Presently the local governments own 11 percent of the 1990 state property, and a further 5 percent of state property is to be privatized in the course of 1997 and 1998. Approximately half of the state property (in market value) has basically disappeared, due to the collapse of Eastern European markets, the unfavorable taxation system, the domestic markets lost following the liberalization of imports, and several other factors. Although liquidation has also played a great role in channeling state property to the private sector (11 percent), the majority of state companies suffered a loss in value without being liquidated. The outcome of Hungarian privatization is shown in figures 10 and 11.

Hungarian privatization has not achieved its initial goals completely. In 1990 the new coalition government tried to sell state property equaling $10 billion quickly, with the intention of reducing the external debt of the country with this amount. Privatization in Hungary reached significant foreign exchange revenues only later, in 1995 ($3 billion), and the total cash revenue did not exceed $7 billion between 1990 and 1996. This is the reason why the external debts could not be reduced substantially by privatization revenues. Another important goal of Hungarian privatization was to create a proprietary group that was supposed to lay down the basis of a new middle class. This goal has only been achieved to a small extent, since the financial allowances provided for domestic investors, managers, and employees were not sufficient to involve domestic investors in Hungarian privatization to a great extent. In my view, the main reason for this is that between 1990 and 1996 the most profitable business for domestic owners

Figure 10

Source: Privatization Research Institute.

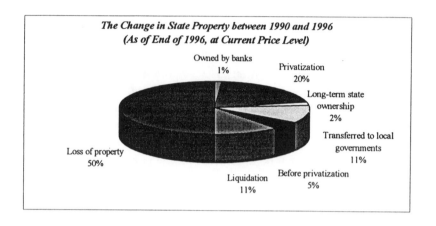

Figure 11

Source: Source: Privatization Research Institute.

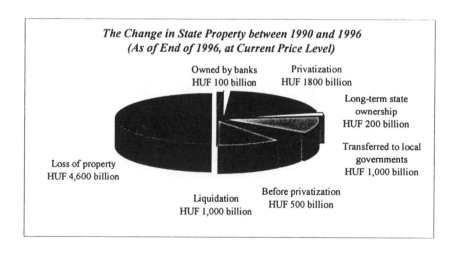

was not the purchase of privatized state property but buying public securities. Public securities yielded a considerably higher profit than buying the assets of a state company.

Also, Hungarian privatization has not entirely achieved its goal of reorganizing the major part of Hungarian industry by selling it to foreign investors. The reason for this is that the foreign investors found Hungarian privatization slow and complicated, and in many cases they preferred greenfield investments to privatization. Of the $15.25 billion FDI flowing into Hungary until the end of 1996, 50 percent was spent on greenfield investments, illustrating this tendency. Naturally, greenfield investments have also greatly contributed to the technological renewal of Hungarian industry; moreover, in the fields of electronics, telecommunications, and especially car manufacturing they established new industries in Hungary.

A further goal of privatizational policy was to provide the newly organized pension schemes with substantial funds deriving from state companies. This goal has again been partly achieved only, which prevented a business sector similar to the most developed OECD countries from coming into being, in which pension funds and pension insurance companies play a significant role.

Among the positive features of Hungarian privatization the following could be pointed out: its relative rapidity, the significant participation of foreign direct capital in the technological renewal of Hungarian economy, the role of the property passed on to the local governments to develop country towns, and a social environment far from hostile that surrounded privatization. However, it is also apparent that this social environment changed in 1996, and in the coming years the vast majority of the population might become ever increasingly critical of Hungarian privatization.

After the completion of privatization it is expected that significant post privatizational processes will take place in the Hungarian economy in the following years. In this respect, the following forecast can be made:

- Privatization will continue after the conclusion of state-controlled processes, through the sale of property owned by local governments. For domestic and foreign investors, this will constitute one of the most important fields of investment.
- As a result of privatization, about thirty to forty large companies have been able to afford a significant restructuring of its products, capital, organization, and management. These companies will also be able to perform well at the BSE in the first place but probably also as the Vienna

91

and New York stock exchanges. It will be worth investing in the shares of these companies, since these companies are market leaders on the domestic market, their exports are continuously increasing, and their new, usually foreign owners continuously invest in them.

- Another result of privatization is that about thirty companies, owned by promising domestic investors, show dynamic development in the business sector in Hungary. After their privatization, the new owners of these companies are the management, employees, domestic banks, financial institutions, and domestic private portfolio investors. These companies stand a good chance of playing a significant role in Hungary and the neighboring countries (the Czech Republic, Slovakia, the Ukraine, Romania, Serbia, and Croatia) and developing into regional multinational companies. Investment into these companies is promising because, beyond the Hungarian market with 10 million people, access can be gained to a further market of 70 to 80 million people through these Hungarian companies.

- A further result of privatization is the termination of the limited capacity of telecommunications and the motorway system in Hungary. This will affect the future development of a "city quadrangle" among Vienna, Budapest, Bratislava, and Brno, which will establish an industrial, service, financial, and trade center in Europe that is similar to the London region, the Paris region, the Lyon region, or the Milan region. Investments arriving in this region will yield an especially high profit in the future.

- Besides privatization, another major form of foreign investment has been the form of greenfield investments. It is expected that, besides the companies already privatized, another supplier-cooperative business sector will develop that promotes imports and also helps these companies enhance their exports. This new cooperative business sector will be created by foreign and domestic greenfield investments. The Hungarian government is expected to provide substantial financial allowances for the development of this new, generally medium-sized company sector. It is also expected that there will be many promising projects for foreign investors in this new business sector.

Appendix: Privatization in the Main Industrial Sectors

The following chart contains the most important state-owned companies participating in privatization, showing the method of privatization.

Enterprise	Privatization method	Date	Name of new owner
INDUSTRY			
Food industry			
Pécs Tobacco Factory	negotiations, agreement with buyer	1991	BAT (British-U.S.)
Debrecen Tobacco Factory	tender	1992	Reemtsma (German)
Kőbánya Brewery	tender	1993	SAB (South African)
Borsod Brewery	tender	1991	Interbrew (Belgian)
Budapest Liquor Company	tender	1991	Zwack consortium
Szerencs Chocolate Factory	negotiations, agreement with buyer	1991	Nestlé
Szabadegyháza Liquor Company	tender	1991	Amylum (Belgian)
Mátravidék Sugar Mill	negotiations, agreement with buyer	1991	Béghin-Say (French)
Szerencs Sugar Mill	negotiations, agreement with buyer	1991	Béghin-Say (French)
Vegetable Oil and Detergent Manufacturing Company	tender	1992	Ferruzzi-Unilever

93

Municipal Mineral Water and Soft Drink Co.	tender	1992	Pepsi Cola
Pick	private and public offering	1992	public floating, foreign institutional investors
Pápa Meat Factory	tender	1993	management, employees, farmers
Zala Meat	tender	1993	management, employees, farmers
Sárvár Poultry Processing	tender	1993	B. Matthews (British)
Barneval (poultry)	liquidation	1994 - 95	Hajdúbét (Hungarian)
Hajdú Milk	private and public offering	1994	1. Nutricia, small-scale investors 2. Friesland (Dutch)
Fejér Milk	tender	1992	Parmalat (Italian)
Hajdú Grain	tender	1993	management, employees, farmers
Buda Mills	tender	1994	Hungarian investors
Globus Canning Factory	private and public offering	1993	foreign institutional investors, public floating
Debrecen Canning Factory	liquidation	1994 - 95	Hungarian investors

Machine industry

Tungsram	negotiations, agreement with buyer	1989	1. Girozentrale 2. General Electric (U.S.)
Láng	partial sale, negotiations with buyer	1989	ABB (Swedish)
Lehel Refrigerator	negotiations, agreement with buyer	1991	Elektrolux (Swedish)
Sopron Elzett Locks	negotiations, agreement with buyer	1991	Roto
Székesfehérvár Light Metal	joint venture, then buyout	1991, 1996	Alcoa (U.S.)
Perion Battery	tender	1993	management, employees
Mofém Metal	tender	1993	Spanish investors
Hajdúsági Iparművek	tender	1994	management
MMG (instruments)	tender	1994	employees
Videoton (electronics)	liquidation	1992, 1996	Hungarian investors
Orion (TV factory)	liquidation	1995	Russian investors
Cable Works	tender	1993	Siemens (German)

Chemical industry

Chinoin (pharmaceutical industry)	negotiations, agreement with buyer	1991	Sanofi (French)
Caola (cosmetics)	tender	1993	Hungarian investors
Egis (pharmaceutical industry)	private and public offering	1993	1. EBRD foreign institutional investors 2. Servier (French)
Richter (pharmaceutical industry)	private and public offering	1994, 1995	foreign institutional investors public company
Borsodchem (plastics)	private and public offering	1996	EBRD (foreign institutional investors)
TVK (plastics)	private and public offering	1996	foreign institutional investors
Taurus (rubber)	tender	1996	Michelin (French)

Printing works

Petőfi Printing Works	negotiations, agreement with buyer	1992	Cofinec
Szikra Printing Works	tender	1995	Postabank, Láng Holding

Furniture industry

Balaton Furniture Factory	tender	1992	Fotex

Paper mills

Dunapack	negotiations, agreement	1990,1995	Prinzhorn (Austrian)
Szolnoki Papírgyár	liquidation	1994, 1995	Austrian investors

Construction material industry

Zalakerámia	public and private offering	1992	foreign institutional investors
Alföld China Factory	tender	1993	Villeroy (German)
brick factories	tender, agreement		Wienerberger (Austrian)
tile factories	tender, agreement		Tondach (Austrian)

Textile industry

Újpest Yarn Factory	negotiations, agreement with buyer	1989	Coats (British)
Styl Apparel	public and private offering	1991	Bäumler, foreign institutional investors, public floating
Gardenia Curtain Factory	negotiations agreement with buyer	1991	foreign professional investors
Sotex (carpets)	tender	1994	Graboplast
Albertfalva Twisting Factory	tender, leasing privatization	1992	Hungarian investors
Szeged Apparel	tender	1993	employees

Pápa Textile Mills	liquidation	1994	Hungarian bank
Latex	liquidation	1994	Hungarian bank
Construction industry			
Magyar Aszfalt	negotiations, agreement with buyer	1989	Bauholding (Austrian)
road building companies	negotiations, agreement with buyer	1989	Strabag (Austrian)
Bridge Construction Co.	tender	1993	French investor
Vegyépszer	tender	1994	management, employees
Public Building Construction Co.	tender	1994	management employees
Magyar Építő	tender	1994	management employees
Metallurgy			
Dunaferr Cold Mill	joint venture	1992	Voest Alpine (Austrian)
December 4 Wire Mill	liquidation agreement	1994	Metaltrade (Hungarian-Slovak)
Agriculture			
Szekszárd Agrocombinate	negotiations, agreement with buyer	1993	German investor
Tokaj Wineries	partial sale negotiations, agreement	1992-95	French, Spanish other investors
Tata State Farm	tender	1992	Hungarian investors
Környe Agrocombinate	tender	1994	Hungarian investors

Commerce

Duna Füszért	negotiations, agreement with buyer	1989	Delhaize (Belgian)
Azur	negotiations, agreement with buyer	1989	Fotex
Compack	tender	1991	Sara Lee (U.S.A.)
Agrimpex	negotiations, agreement with buyer	1992	British investor
Keravill	tender	1992	1. Technoimpex 2. Fotex
Mogürt	tender	1992	management
Csemege	tender, negotiations	1992	Julius Meinl (Austrian)
Budapest Agroker	tender	1993	Intercooperation (U.S.)
Amfora	tender	1993	management
Centrum	tender	1994	management employees
Budapest Közért	tender	1994	Israeli investor
Kisalföld Füszért	tender	1994	management

Hotel industry

Pannonia Hotels	tender	1993	Accor (French)
Danubius	public and private offering	1992	foreign institutional investors
Forum Hotel	tender	1996	Intercontinental

Transportation

Malév	tender, joint venture	1993-94	Alitalia

Telecommunication

Matáv	tender	1993, 1995	Deutsche Telekom, Ameritech

Financial sector

Hungaria Insurance	negotiations, agreement with buyer	1989	Allianz (German)
State Insurance	tender	1992	Aegon (Dutch)
Foreign Trade Bank	tender	1994	Bayerische Landesbank
OTP	partial privatization public and private offering	1995	public company
Budapest Bank	tender	1995	G.E. Capital EBRD
Credit Bank	tender	1996	ABN-AMRO

Source: Privatization Research Institute.

Bibliography

I   Party Programs, Political Evaluations

*Agrarian Federation – The Civil Agrarian Party. Election Program.*Budapest: Agrarian

Federation, 1994. pp. 45-47.

FIATAL DEMOKRATÁK SZÖVETSÉGE. *Enterprise and Growth. Economic Program of*

FIDESZ. Budapest: FIDESZ, 1994. pp. 58-63.

FIATAL DEMOKRATÁK SZÖVETSÉGE. *Enterprise and Growth. The Economic Program*

of FIDESZ. Budapest: 1993. FIDESZ, pp. 28-34.

FIATAL DEMOKRATÁK SZÖVETSÉGE. *Program Approved By the 2nd Congress of the*

Young Democrats. Budapest: FIDESZ, 1989. p.91.

FIATAL DEMOKRATÁK SZÖVETSÉGE. *The Economic, Social and Agricultural Program*

of FIDESZ. Budapest: FIDESZ, 1993. pp. 52-53.

FIATAL DEMOKRATÁK SZÖVETSÉGE. *Vote for a Better Future! Election Message of*

FIDESZ. Budapest: FIDESZ, April 1994. pp. 28-31 .

FIATAL DEMOKRATÁK SZÖVETSÉGE.*Vote For the Better Future! Election Program.*

Budapest: FIDESZ, 1990. P.31

FÜGGETLEN KISGAZDA FÖLDMUNKÁS ÉS POLGÁRI PÁRT .*Our Past, Present and*

Future. Election Program of the Independent Small Farmer, Agrarian Worker And Civil

Party (FKGP) For The Turn Of The Millennium. Budapest: 1992. pp. 25-28.

FÜGGETLEN KISGAZDA FÖLDMUNKÁS ÉS POLGÁRI PÁRT .*Our Past, Present,*

Future. Election Program. Budapest: FKGP, 1993. pp. 20-22.

KERESZTÉNYDEMOKRATA NÉPPÁRT. *KDNP Election Program.*Budapest: KDNP, 1994. pp. 41-43.

MAGYAR DEMOKRATA FÓRUM. *Actions and Tasks. Five Years of MDF.* Budapest: MDF, 1993. pp. 50-59.

MAGYAR DEMOKRATA FÓRUM. Program of the Democratic Forum (MDF). Budapest: Front, 1989. pp. 159-164.

MAGYAR DEMOKRATA FÓRUM. *Sure Steps, Safe Future. MDF Program.*Budapest: MDF, 1994. pp. 141-142.

MAGYAR SZOCIALISTA PÁRT. *Challenges and Answers. 1994-1998 Election Program. Professional Chapters.* Budapest: MSZP, 1994. pp. 284-286.

MAGYAR SZOCIALISTA PÁRT. *Hungary at the Turn of the Millennium.* Budapest: MSZP, 1993. pp. 15-19.

MAGYAR SZOCIALISTA PÁRT. *Principles, Facts, Arguments. Additional Material to the Election Program of the Socialists.* Budapest: MSZP, 1990. pp. 101-102.

MAGYAR SZOCIALISTA PÁRT. *There is the Better Way! Socialists on Economy, Society and Politics.* Budapest: MSZP, 1992. pp. 168-190.

MAGYAR SZOCIALISTA PÁRT.*For a Modern Democratic Hungary (Draft of the Short-term Political Program of MSZP).* Budapest: MSZP, 1993. pp. 13-18.

Program Of National Rebirth. Budapest: FKGP, 1990. pp. 50-63.

Program of National Renewal. The First Three Years of the Republic. Budapest: September 1990. pp. 198-202.

SZABAD DEMOKRATÁK SZÖVETSÉGE. *Program of the Change of Regime.* Budapest:
Free Democrats (SZDSZ), 1989. pp. 143-160.

SZABAD DEMOKRATÁK SZÖVETSÉGE. *SZDSZ on Privatization and Compensation.*
Budapest: SZDSZ, 1991. pp. 21-34.

SZABAD DEMOKRATÁK SZÖVETSÉGE. *The Liberal Solution. Crisis Management
Program of SZDSZ.* Budapest: SZDSZ, 1991. pp. 132-181.

SZABAD DEMOKRATÁK SZÖVETSÉGE. *Union of Free Democrats – Economic Policy.
SZDSZ Election Program.* Budapest: SZDSZ, 1994. pp. 12-38.

*Whom To Elect, Who To Vote For? Election Information (The Compendium Of The
Programs Of Political Parties Participating In The 1990 Election Press Campaign In
Hungary)* Budapest, Pack-Art, 1990. pp. 45-89.

Documents, Official Evaluations

" Act No. 6 Of 1990 On the Public Floating and Allocation of Certain Securities and The Security Exchange. " *Official Gazette* 13 (1990): 228-62.

"Act No. 33 Of 1991 On the Transfer of Certain State-Owned Assets to Municipality Ownership." *Official Gazette* 87 (1991): 1829-52.

"Act No. 44 of 1992 on ESOP." *Official Gazette* 69 (1992): 234-38.

"Act No. 49 of 1991 on Bankruptcy, Liquidation and Final Settlement." *Official Gazette* 117 (1991): 2311-25.

"Act No. 53 of 1992 on the Management and Utilization of State-Owned Assets Remaining Permanently in State Hands." *Official Gazette* 81 (1992): 2653-60.

"Act No. 54 of 1992 on the Evaluation, Utilization and Protection of Assets in Temporary State Ownership (August 1992)." *Official Gazette* 81 (1992): 2660-73.

"Act No. 55 of 1992 on the Amendment of Regulations Relating to the Laws on State-Owned Assets." *Official Gazette* 81 (1992): 2673-83

"Act No. 6 of 1977 on State-Owned Enterprises and Decree No. 33." Issued on October 31, 1984 by the Council of Ministers on the Execution of the Former, Compiled as a Uniform Structure and with Explanations by the Minister. *Official Gazette* special issue, 30(1990): 7-27.

"Act No. 6 of 1988 on Business Entities and All Amendments Compiled as a Uniform Structure." *Official Gazette* 143 (1991): 2917-55.

"Act No. 74 Of 1990 On The Privatization (Sale, Utilization) Of Assets Of State-Owned Enterprises Performing Retail, Catering And Consumer Service Activity." *Official Gazette* 95 (1990): 1886-94.

"Act No. 86 Of 1990 On the Prohibition of Unfair Market Behavior." *Official Gazette* 21(1990): 2361-83.

"Act No. 25 of 1991 on Compensation." August 10, 1991.

Csorba, János. *White Book on Hungarian Transition.* Budapest: Ownership Foundation–Privatization Research Institute, 1992.

GKI Economic Research Company Studies. Budapest: GKI, 1990-95.

Prime Minister's Office–Economic Policy Secretariat. Enterprise Management, Privatization, Competition Policy. 1990.

Compensation Methods (studies): Budapest: Privatization Society, 1994.

Privatization Strategic Work Group: *The Breakthrough Concept and Government Work Program of Privatization.* 1992. PRIVINFO Year Book 1992.Budapest: State Property Agency, 1993.

Privatization Strategy of the Government. 1994.

PRIVINFO vols. 1-5. Budapest: State Property Agency, 1992-96.

PRIVINFO Year Book 1993. State Property Agency, 1994.

Report on Hungarian Privatization 1991. Budapest: Ownership Foundation–Privatisation Research Institute, 1992.

Report on Hungarian Privatization 1993. Budapest: Ownership Foundation–Privatisation Research Institute, 1994.

1993 Business Plan. Budapest: State Privatization and Property Holding Company, 1993.

Annual Report 1993. Budapest: State Privatization and Property Holding Company, 1994.

The Institutional Regulatory Background of Privatization 'Legal Summary'. Budapest: State Property Agency, 1994.

The Status of Privatization, Budapest: State Property Agency, 1994.

Varga, Károly. *Legislation Preparatory Action Research on Privatization.* Budapest: Industrial Institute 1992.

Antal, László. "A Subjective Opinion on Transition." *Társadalmi Szemle* 4 (1992). 3-11.

Árvay, János and Vértes, András. *The Private Sector and the Weight of Hidden Economy in Hungary 1980-1992*. Budapest: 1994. pp. 210-212.

Auth Henrik, and Járai Zsigmond. "Showing the Tracks." *HVG*, November 25, 1989.

Auth, Henrik. "The Redistribution of Economic Power Has Begun."

Auth, Henrik and Krokos, János. "Suspicious transformations." *Figyelő* February 9, 1989.

Bálint, Tamás. *Ownership of the Municipalities*. Budapest: Agrocent, 1991. P.205

Bank And Loan Consolidation, Bank Privatization (studies). Budapest: Privatization Society 1994. P.66

Bokros, Lajos. "Dirty Things are to Happen Here." *Beszélő* February 5, 1990.

Capital Market and Privatization in Eastern Europe. CHALLENGES, Academy Global Economy Research Institute. 1993.

Development of the Social Market Economy and the Private Economy in Hungary (conference study volume). Adenauer Foundation–SPA, 1994.

Experience of Privatization in Eastern Central Europe. CHALLENGES, Academy Global Economy Research Institute, 1993.

Figyelő November 23, 1989.

Foreign Direct Investments in Hungary, Modernization Effects and Short-Term Perspectives.
CHALLENGES, Academy Global Economy Research Institute, 1995.

Gács, János. "Liberalization of Foreign Trade in Eastern Europe-Fast Reforms and a Review:
Experiences in Poland and Hungary." *Külgazdaság* 12 (1993): 12-33.

Hamar, János. "FDI and Privatization in Hungary."

Herczeg, János. "One Form of Privatization-the Foreign-Owned Company: Strategies,
Effects, Contradictions." *Gazdaság és társadalom* 3 (1993): 83-102.

International Experience of Privatizing the Bank System. CHALLENGES, Academy Global
Economy Research Institute, 1992.

International Scientific Conference: *Privatization in Eastern Europe.* Geneva: UNO-
Development and Commercial Institute and Budapest: Kopint-Datorg, 1993.

Kerek, Zoltán. *Bankruptcy, Liquidation, Reorganization.* Budapest: KJK, 1992. P.175

Kornai, János. "The Socialist System-A Critical Political Economy." Budapest: HVG, 1993.

Kornai, János. "Principles of Privatization in Eastern Europe." *Közgazdasági Szemle* 11
(1991): 1021-40.

Kornai, János. "The Liquidation of the Economy of Shortages–General Analysis and a
Review of Hungarian Development." *Közgazdasági Szemle* 7-8 (1994): 569-605.

Krasznai, Zoltán. *Privatization in Hungary-Conference on Transformation in Eastern
Europe.* Prague: 1994. P.20

Krokos, János. "Entrepreneur Competition instead of Performance Bargaining!"
Közgazdasági Szemle 7-8 (1988).

Laky, Tamás. "The Creation of Private Economy and Employment." *Közgazdasági Szemle* 7-8 (1995): 685-709.

Lengyel, László and Matolcsy, György. *The Ownership Reform.* Budapest: Financial Research Company, 1988.

Lengyel, László. *History of Ownership Disputes and the Reform.* Budapest: Financial Research Company, 1988.

Mass Privatization Dilemmas in the Light of the Present Status of Household Savings and Capital Markets. CHALLENGES, Academy Global Economy Research Institute. 1994.

Matolcsy, György. "From State Enterprise to Joint Ownership." *Valóság* 6 (1988).

Matolcsy, György. "In the Trap of Eight and a Half Illusions." *Figyelő* May 25, 1989.

Matolcsy, György. *Privatization on Half Way.* Budapest: 1995. P.113

Matolcsy, György. *Variations on the Ownership Reform.* Budapest: Financial Research Company, 1988.

Nádudvari, Zoltán. "International Practice of Bankruptcy Statistics." *Gazdaságstatisztika* 4 (1992): 60-66.

Nagy, Attila. "Transition – From Where to Where?" *Valóság* 9 (1993): 1-18.

Nyers, Rezsö. and Pap, János. "Privatization in the Hungarian Bank System." *Bankszemle* 3-4 (1992): 1-11.

Report on Hungarian Privatization–First Six Months of 1994. Budapest: Ownership Foundation–PRI, 1994. P.261

109

Román, Zoltán. "International Experience of Privatization." *Kereskedelmi Szemle* 6 (1992): 33-42.

Sárközi, Tamás. *In the Wake of an Economic Organizational Reform*. Budapest: Magvető, 1986. P.367

Soós, Károly Attila. "Privatization, Self-Government Free of Dogmas and the Ownership Reform." *Közgazdasági Szemle* 7-8 (1989).

Szamuely, László. "Privatization in the Transforming Central and Eastern Europe."

Tardos, Márton. "Business Organizations and Ownership." *Gazdaság* 3 (1988).

Tardos, Márton. "Elimination of State Ownership–Why and How." *Ipargazdaság* 1 (1992): 8-13.

Tardos, Márton. Elimination of State Ownership-Why and How." *Külgazdaság* 12 (1991).

Tardos, Márton.: "The Ownership." *Közgazdasági Szemle* 12 (1989).

The Economic Price of German Reunification. CHALLENGES, Academy Global Economy Research Institute, 1992.

The Role of Bankruptcy in the Economic Transformation of Eastern Central Europe. CHALLENGES, Academy Global Economy Research Institute. 1993.

The Role of Foreign Capital in Privatization. CHALLENGES, Academy Global Economy Research Institute. 1994.

Research Papers, Professional Evaluations

Amortization and Investment Replacement Shortage – 2d Debate Material. PRI, 1995.

Amortization and Investment Replacement Shortage. PRI, 1995.

Árva, László. *Direct Foreign Investments: Some Theoretical and Parctical Issues.* 1995.

Capital Loss in Hungary in the 1989-1996 Period. PRI, 1996.

Compensation and Privatization. PRI, 1994..

Economic Transformation and Privatization. Privatization Research Institute, 1991.

Effect of Privatization Processes on the Functioning of the Economy. PRI, 1991.

Environment of Privatization Economic Policy. PRI, 1992.

German-Hungarian Industrial Cooperation on the Company Level (expert evaluation and interviews). PRI, 1995.

Hungarian Foreign Trade and Industrial Competitive Advantages. PRI, 1995.

Kopátsy, Sándor. *Choosing the Wrong Economic policy. PRI,* 1993.

Kopátsy, Sándor. *Economy of the Consumer Society. PRI,* 1993.

Kopátsy, Sándor. *More Light! CET,* May 1995.

Kopátsy, Sándor. There is the Way Out! *Belvárosi,* 1995.

Kopátsy, Sándor. *There is the Way Out! CET,* July 1995.

Kopátsy, Sándor. *Our 20th Century. Belvárosi,* 1996.

111

Marking Time and Free Fall–Hungarian Economy and Society in 1996 and Forecasts for 1997. PRI 1996.

Matolcsy, György. "Adjustment and Recession." *Közgazdasági Szemle* September 1997.

Matolcsy, György. "Avidity and Love." *Kritika* 1997.

Matolcsy, György. "Conspiracy or Coincidence?" *Kritika* June 1996.

Matolcsy, György. "Economic and Social Shock Therapies." *Társadalmi Szemle* May 1996.

Matolcsy, György. "Original Capital Reallocation in Hungary" (operation of Capital Pumps in the 1990's). *Századvég* 1997.

Matolcsy, György. "The Culpable Model Pupil." *Kritika* 1996.

Matolcsy, György. *Anatomy of the Economic Change of Regime.* PRI, 1996.

Matolcsy, György. *The Drama Itself.* HVG, 1996.

Matolcsy, György. *What Economic Policy for the European Union?* PRI, 1996.

Privatisation on Half Way. PRI, 1995.

Privatization in Hungary. PRI 1997.

Privatization, Ownership Restructuring and Company Founding–Report on the First Six Months. 1993. PRI, 1993.

Privatization, Receivership, Lliquidation and Employment. PRI, 1992.

Report on Hungarian Privatization. 1993. PRI, 1994.

Sebestyén, Tamás. *Adjusted Balance Sheet data of MOL Company for the 1992-1996 period.*

Study prepared in the PRI by appointment of MOL Company, Budapest, May 1996.

Sebestyén, Tamás. *Adjusted Balance Sheet Data of TVK Company for the 1992-1996 period.* Study prepared in the PRI by appointment of TVK Company, Budapest, April 1996.

Sebestyén, Tamás. *Amortization Replacement Shortage of Power Companies in the 1992-1995 period.* Study prepared in the PRI by appointment of MVM Company, Budapest, August 1996.

Sebestyén, Tamás. *Capital Loss in Hungary in the 1989-1996 period.* Study prepared in the PRI by appointment of OMFB (vols. 1-3.), Budapest, October 1996.

Sebestyén, Tamás. *Capital Loss in the 1992-1995 period in the Power Industry.* Hungarian Power Authority Bulletin, 1997, no.1, pp. 14-24.

Sebestyén, Tamás. "Shortage of Amortization Replacement and Investments." *MÁS—KÉP(P)* periodical of the Trade Union Economy and Social Research Institute, Budapest, December 1995, pp. 31-61.

Status of Hungarian Privatization and Administration of State Ownership. PRI, 1995.

The Balance of the Hungarian Privatization 1990-1993. PRI, 1994.

The Past Two Years of Privatization. PRI, 1992.

The Review of Small and Medium-Size Enterprises Participating in Privatization (facts and assumptions). PRI, 1995.

The State of the Hungarian Industry in 1995. PRI, 1995.